Reston Publishing Company, Inc.
Reston, Virginia
A Prentice-Hall Company

Gretchen Mann Andersen

CREATIVE EXPLORATION IN CRAFTS

Library of Congress Cataloging in Publication Data

Andersen, Gretchen Mann, 1933-
  Creative exploration in crafts.

  Bibliography: p.
  Includes index.
  1. Handicraft. I. Title.
TT157.A55   745.5   75-38762
ISBN 0-87909-169-X
ISBN 0-87909-168-1 pbk.

© 1976 by Reston Publishing Company, Inc.
A Prentice-Hall Company
Reston, Virginia

10 9 8 7 6 5 4 3 2 1

Printed in the United States of America

CONTENTS

PREFACE

If you are an explorer, a curiosity seeker, a cultivator of the unusual, this book was written for you. Hopefully, you will find between the covers of this book a new unexplored terrain that will challenge you. The terrain is the world of crafts, and this book attempts to guide you at the outset of your journey into this world. It does not pretend to be complete in its coverage, but it is meant to show you many of the beautiful facets of the world of crafts. It is up to you to search further in workshops, museums, craft shops around the world, and in other books for more in-depth information on your favorite craft areas.

The acknowledgements for a book of this type are extensive. Since I am a faculty member of Kapiolani Community College, I must first thank all those with whom I work who have helped me in hidden ways to complete this book: Dr. Frederick Haehnlen, my Provost; Harriet Nakamoto, my Dean of Instruction; James Jeffreys, my division chairman; Robert Fearrien, my department chairman and office mate; Charles Bretz, Carol Langner, Jeanne Wiig, my art colleagues; Myrna Gayle Barenz and her occupational therapy students, and all of my craft students and friends who helped me as models and permitted me to photograph their work, especially: Marilyn Ambrosio, Naomi Beals, Tracy Doolittle, Karen Enos, Denise Go, Brenda Ha, Loretta Hicks, Torsie Hoe, Linda Husereau, Gary Iseri, Beverly Khan, Jo Ann Lum, Nolan Miguel, Laurie Miyamoto, Marquis Miyauchi, Kathleen Miyamura, Roy Ono, Keith Smith, Francis Soberano, Wendy Stanton, Jaime Stone, Julie Sugitan, Richard Takashima, Donna Woish, and Nora Yasatomi.

As a craftsman I wish to acknowledge with sincere appreciation the many other craftsmen who assisted me by providing suggestions on the various chapters and by permitting me to photograph their works: Anna Ballerian (Tie Dye), Jerome Wallace (Batik), Jean Williams (Weaving), Martie Rhodes (Enameling), Charles Bretz (Ceramics), Carol Langner (Textile Silk Screening), and Myrna Gayle Barenz (Leathercraft).

A sincere appreciation is extended to Virginia Greenberg, a research chemist at the University of Hawaii who checked the definitions involving chemistry in the Glossary; Masa Nakano and Robert Fearrien who assisted me in proofreading this manuscript; the photographic team at Laurence Hata's in Honolulu who processed my film and prints so carefully; and all of the many suppliers who are listed in Appendix B who besides permitting me to list them in this book, also, in many cases, supplied me with valuable suggestions.

Lastly, I wish to extend my sincerest *mahalo* to the many people who encouraged me to write this book: Weldon Rackley who read and responded to my many letters about the project, and Joseph Murray, Reston Publishing Company's representative, without whom this book would never have seen the light of day.

Gretchen Mann Andersen

one
INTRODUCTION

The basic idea behind this book is to provide simple, graphic illustrations that will guide the beginning craftsman or student in an exploration of some of the major craft areas. Besides providing easy directions on how to work with various media, each chapter lists supplies and sources of supplies as well as some further suggestions as to other ideas that can be pursued in each medium. Suggestions are also given for combining materials from different crafts, because the use of more than one medium can greatly enhance and enrich an object. Each chapter is meant to be a "beginning." Further sources of information are listed under each craft area in the bibliography.

The chapter on *Designing a Craft Object* presents some very basic ideas with regard to design and the use of the art elements in craft objects. Since the design of a craft object is of major importance, you should plan to do a thorough study of design in each craft area. Reading books and magazines, looking into the historical development and accomplishments in your craft areas, attending craft shows and studying award winning works will aquaint you with good design qualities and craft techniques. Try contacting other craftsmen; they are usually delighted to discuss their techniques with someone who is interested in their work.

The crafts discussed in this book were chosen because they are the ones that most people would like to learn something about. Each craft provides its own challenges and delights. The excitement of opening a birthday present is found in many crafts; for example, untying the strings or threads of a tie-dyed piece, watching an enameled piece cool to its final coloration, and opening a kiln after a glaze firing.

Often there are disappointments—the dye does not go where you want it to go in a tie dye, the enamel cracks, a ceramic piece shatters in the kiln—but you can turn disappointments into challenges. Never be stopped by your failures. It takes time to do something well, and it takes ages, it seems, to do something perfectly. But the joy of accomplishment has that much more meaning when you work hard for it. You never really appreciate a craft until you try to do it. It is expected that some of your first projects will not turn out well; others, however, will be very successful. Try over again at a later date a project or a craft that does not seem to work. *Explore!* Keep the doors open! Often the craft that has been a fiasco to begin with ends up being the craft that you will enjoy the most because it is the most challenging, and because it has so many variables.

By going to craft shows and visiting craft stores, you can pick up many ideas in your craft areas. Let yourself be inspired by different approaches. Enjoy your journey into the world of crafts. Hopefully this book will be for you a beginning of a lifetime of joy and accomplishment in the crafts.

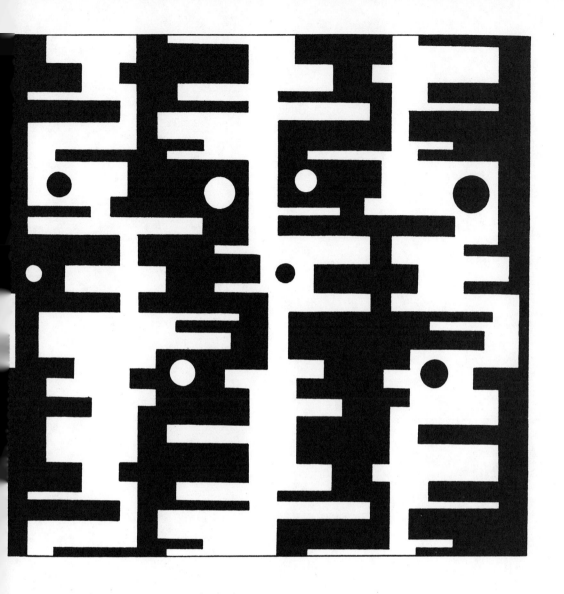

two

DESIGNING
A CRAFT OBJECT

Chapter opening shows alternated positive-negative space.

A craft object can be either functional or nonfunctional; it may perform no other function than that of being visually and aesthetically pleasing. Whether you are creating functional or nonfunctional objects, you should know a few principles of design and understand how to use the art elements when creating a craft object.

DESIGNING

Many craft objects consist not only of a shape or a form but also of a design that has been placed on that shape or form. Sometimes a motif (a single design) can be repeated to create a rhythm on the surface of an object. Figure 2-1 shows the use of a repeated design that can be used on woven, tie-dyed, batik, or silkscreened fabric, or on a ceramic surface. In a repeated motif, you can alternate your design as shown in Figure 2-2 by turning every other design upside down; you can drop your design at half step intervals as shown in Figure 2-3; you can alternate positive-negative space as shown in the chapter opening illustration; or you can alternate two designs with each other as

Figure 2-1. A repeated single motif.

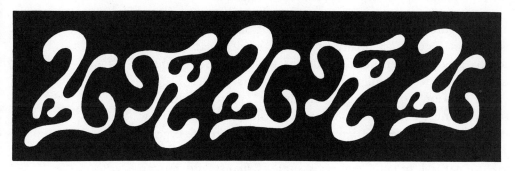

Figure 2-2. Alternated single motif.

Figure 2-3. Half-step-dropped motif.

Figure 2-4. Alternated repeated design with two motifs.

shown in figure 2-4. You may also vary the size of your motif as shown in Figure 2-5. Many of the above ideas can be combined to produce even more variations. Visiting yardage shops to study fabric designs will suggest further ideas.

In addition to creating a rhythmical pattern with the motif, you must decide on the design of the motif itself. How do you begin to create a design unit? Basically, there are organic and geometric shapes that can be considered. Organic shapes relate to natural organic materials such as plants and human beings, while geometric shapes are constructed with the help of ruler, compass, and mechanical devices.

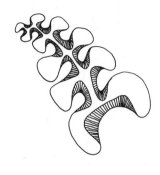

Figure 2-5. Design of various sized motifs.

Figure 2-6. Organically shaped motif based on a growth pattern of leaves.

In creating an organic shape, consider a design in terms of a growth pattern. Figure 2-6 shows the larger units at the bottom with the smaller units at the top. Curving, flowing lines as shown in Figure 2-7 are also organic. Consider an amoeba with its ability to pull in and push out various sections of its form in order to enclose food particles or to move (Figure 2-8). This form, as seen in Figure 2-9, has great possibilities when combined with some of the previous ideas. This type of organic design is often referred to as a free form design.

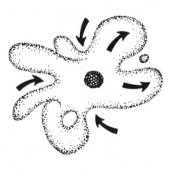

Figure 2-7. Organic lines.

Figure 2-8. Amoeba enclosing a food particle. Arrows show direction of movement.

Figure 2-9. An organic form incorporating the growth pattern seen in Figure 2-6 and the amoeba form seen in Figure 2-8.

Pleasing motifs can also be developed with geometric lines and shapes. The simple cross shape has possibilities by itself or it can be developed further as a radial design as shown in Figure 2-10. A radial design is a design that radiates from a central point like the spokes of a wheel radiate from the axle.

Symmetrical organic (Figure 2-11) or symmetrical geometric shapes can be made by following these steps:

Figure 2-10 Geometric radial design developed from a simple cross shape.

1. Place a carbon paper on a piece of paper with the carbon side facing the paper.
2. Fold the paper in half so that the carbon paper is on the inside. Draw a design next to the fold of the paper.
3. Open the paper and remove the carbon. You now have a design that is a mirror image on either side of the fold—a symmetrical design.

Figure 2-11. A symmetrical organic design.

An abstract design is a simplified version of an object in which concentration has been placed on the basic form and details have been eliminated. Figure 2-12 shows some objects and the abstract designs that can be developed from them. The wood rose design on the far right is the most abstract of the three designs.

Figure 2-13 shows a nonobjective design. This design has no basis in reality but is a free development by the artist. Some free forms are nonobjective designs.

Figure 2-12. Abstract designs developed from objects shown beneath them.

Figure 2-13. A nonobjective design.

Many of the previously mentioned design ideas can be applied to designing a three-dimensional craft object. As in the previous designs, three-dimensional designs may be organic—as shown in Figure 2-14, geometric—as shown in Figure 2-15, free form—as shown in Figure 2-16, symmetrical—as shown in Figure 2-17, abstract—as shown in Figure 2-18, or nonobjective—as shown in Figure 2-19. There are five basic geometric forms that you can build a design on: the sphere, the cylinder, the cone, the cube, and the pyramid. You can combine and vary these basic forms to create other geometric forms: Figure 2-20 shows a lantern that is a variation of a cube, and Figure 2-21 shows a ceramic vase that is a combination of a cone and a cylinder.

Figure 2-14. Organically designed pin designed by the author and executed by Dr. Robert Coleman.

Figure 2-15. Geometrically designed container in clay created by Charles Bretz.

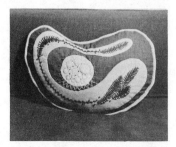

Figure 2-16. Free form decorator pillow created by the author.

Figure 2-17. Symmetrically designed chalice in clay created by Charles Bretz.

Figure 2-18. Abstract pin of cast dental repair acrylic created by the author.

Figure 2-19. Nonobjective pendant in clay created by the author.

Figure 2-20. A ceramic lantern of geometric form based on the square. Created by Charles Bretz.

Figure 2-21. Ceramic vase consisting of a cone and a cylinder. Created by Charles Bretz.

Besides two- and three-dimensional designs, the texture, the color, and the variation of light and dark of an object should also be taken into consideration. These factors combine to contribute to the psychological impact of the object.

Texture

Texture is very similar to, but different from, pattern. Texture is the surface variation of an object, whereas pattern is a repeated motif. However, it is possible for a pattern to create a texture on the surface of a material such as clay, metal, or a woven fabric. Texture is visually indicated by the variation of light falling on or reflected from the surface of an object. A rough texture can sometimes create a psychological feeling of warmth. For example, the rough texture of a rya rug on the floor creates a feeling of warmth as contrasted with the cold feeling communicated by the shiny surface of a highly polished linoleum floor. Rough texture may be used sparingly to create contrast in a craft object, or it may be used extensively to create a rugged, earthy quality in a piece. A smooth, shiny object may communicate a sophisticated, dignified feeling.

If you are photographing your craft object, select a background texture that will contrast with it and enhance it. A rugged texture beneath a shiny object contrasts with and enhances the shiny quality of the object: placing shiny objects in sand will provide such a contrast. A smooth, matte finished object can be favorably contrasted against a roughly textured background. Roughly textured objects will, in turn, be enhanced by being placed on smooth matte surfaces.

Color

Ideas and feelings can also be communicated through color. The influence of Scandinavian color and Pop Art color on our culture has contributed to the feeling that bright, intense colors are "modern," while the back-to-nature movement and the idea of truth to one's materials have contributed to the feeling that "earthy" colors are right for clay, weaving, or macramé. Whole generations of craftsmen have been influenced by the colors of their cultures, but today we have the marvelous legacy of this historical development of color available to us. We can, with the correct choice of colors, recreate the particular mood or feeling of a different culture or a different time period. We are fortunate not to be locked in to definite color patterns. We are free to choose from the past, the present, and to explore new combinations and expressions of colors. We can use the rich rust and dark brown and beige of American Samoa in a textile design to communicate a feeling of primitive art, or we can use turquoise, red coral, and gold colors in enameled jewelry to emphasize an Egyptian-style pendant. We can use bright magentas, oranges, and pinks to give a contemporary feeling to our batik wall hanging, or we can use rusts, browns, and navy blue and white to recreate the feeling of a batik from Java. We may choose to be more conservative and create objects that blend well with the rest of the colors in our homes by doing them in one of the basic "decorator colors" of harvest gold or avocado green, or we may wish to communicate a feeling of earthiness by using the natural colors of the materials used to create our craft object.

Some colors work together better than others. For example, golds seem to work well with browns, beiges, rusts, and oranges, while eggshell blues, blue and green turquoises, and bright greens work well together. Beige, orange, and brown work well together because they are closely related in color, being nearly monochromatic. A *monochromatic* color scheme would be made up of the tints and shades of one color. Light blue, blue, and navy blue would be a monochromatic color scheme. Blue, blue green, and green work well together because they are analogous colors. An *analogous* color scheme would be made up of three or more colors that are next to each other on the color wheel. Yellow orange, orange, and red orange would be an example of an analogous color scheme. Some colors, such as rust brown and turquoise, go well together because they are complementary colors (rust brown is a variation of red orange and turquoise is a variation of blue green). *Complementary* colors are colors that are directly opposite each other on the color wheel and can be found by drawing a line from one color through the center point of the color wheel to the color on the opposite side. *Triadic* colors are colors that are an equal distance apart from each other on the color wheel. If you were to draw an equilateral triangle in the center of the color wheel, the three points of the triangle would indicate a triadic color scheme. Red, yellow, and blue are triadic colors. The above examples are illustrated in Figure 2-22.

The environment in which the colored object is placed is important. The colored background of a craft object can enhance its beauty. A brown object against a brown background looks dull, but a bright orange background will make the object more eyecatching. Background colors can be selected on the basis of some of the color schemes mentioned in the preceding paragraph.

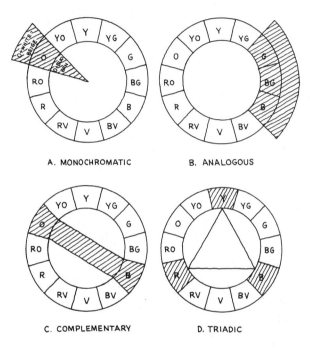

A. MONOCHROMATIC

B. ANALOGOUS

C. COMPLEMENTARY

D. TRIADIC

Figure 2-22. Various Color Schemes: A. Monochromatic; B. Analogous; C. Complementary; D. Triadic.

Light

As with color and texture, the key to good use of light is the use of contrast and subtle degrees of variation. Textures on objects reflect light in a variety of ways. Areas that are concave, or recessed, catch shadows; areas that are convex, or raised, catch the light. A shiny surface will reflect light while a matte surface will create a muted and subtle tonal variation. Exciting things happen when a surface combines smooth and rough textures or concave and convex areas because this creates contrast between light and dark. It is not necessary that your object be both shiny and dull; it can be a piece with simple lines, bright colors, and a shiny surface to emphasize a modern feeling. A piece that has "earthy" colors and shows truth to the materials, such as a clay piece or a wood carving, might look best with a rough texture that creates a muted light reflection. If a piece is primitive, the use of high contrast could be very dramatic; for example, using white against dark brown in a textile. A ceramic surface that has a variety of depths, creating shadows of different values, communicates a sense of mystery. In textiles or two-dimensional surfaces this sense of mystery can be communicated by using transparent layers of color on top of each other, thus enriching the surface with a variety of visual depths. In stitchery and macramé work, several different embroidery stitches or knots can be used to vary the light pattern on the surface of the piece.

CONCLUSION

Attention to design and the art elements can affect the beauty and quality of your craft piece. In the following chapters you will find further suggestions in design and the use of the art elements in specific crafts. These suggestions are made with the hope that you will experiment on your own and develop your own methods for communicating your ideas in the crafts.

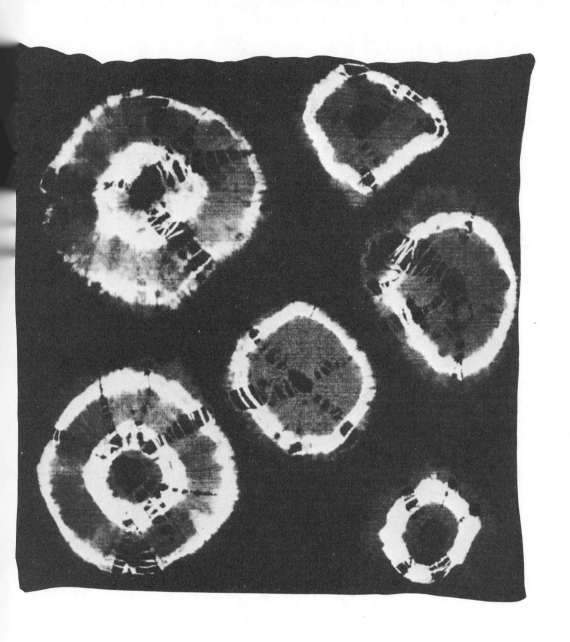

three
TIE DYEING

Chapter opening shows a gathered tie dyed pillow by the author. Two dye baths were used on yellow fabric: one of green and one of navy blue (which became a dark green due to the yellow fabric).

The basic idea behind tie dyeing is that an area of fabric is covered or tied up with twine or fabric strips in order to prevent the dye from entering that area of the fabric when it is placed in the dye. There are many different ways of doing this. The fabric can be knotted or tied on itself; pulled up into a point, tied with twine and dyed; folded, tied with twine or strips of cloth and dyed; or sewn, and the fabric gathered along the thread line, the thread knotted, and then the fabric dyed. The last two methods will be explained in this chapter.

Depending on the effect you want to create, you can tie dye fabrics once or several times. When many dyes are used, the tied areas are usually untied and retied in different places to allow a mixing and an overlapping of colors, so a tie dyed piece that has been dyed many times is very rich in color. When dyeing a piece many colors, start with the lightest color first, such as yellow, and then work down to the middle colors, such as red, to the dark colors, such as blue. This will prevent the dye color in the dye vat from becoming discolored by the deeper colored dyes bleeding into the dye vat.

Discharge dyeing is a process in which a colored fabric is usually used. Fabric ties, twine, or sewn thread that has been

A sewn and gathered tie dye dress created by Torsie Hoe

Accordian pleated dress designed by Nora Yasatomi— two separate dye baths were used.

tied on the fabric will preserve the original color when the fabric is bleached or the dye is discharged.

In order to achieve subtle variations of dye, do not tie the fabric too tightly; tie it securely enough, however, so that the fabric will not become unraveled or untied. By practice and experimenting you will learn to achieve the desired effect.

SUPPLIES

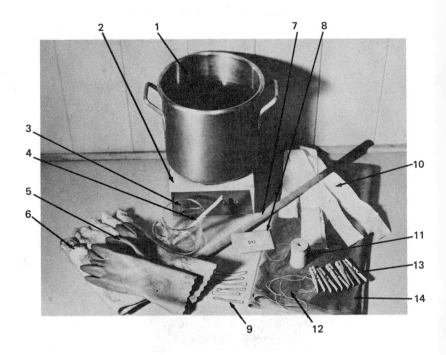

FOLDED TIE DYE

In the folded tie dye technique, fabric is folded and then tied with twine or cloth strips to prevent the dye from entering the fabric. The accordian pleat fold is used vertically here, but you might like to experiment by folding your fabric in halves, fourths, and eighths, into rectangles, or diagonally into diamond shapes before you tie and dye it. The accordian pleat is used so that the dye evenly penetrates all the edges of the fabric. If, however, you plan to make a wall hanging, you may not desire such an even effect and then you could fold the folds into each other, which would result in less dye entering the fabric on the interior of the folded area.

Supplies	Sources of Supplies*
1. Stainless steel or enameled pot	
2. Hot plate or stove	
3. Measuring cup	
4. Chopsticks	
5. Rubber gloves	
6. Asbestos gloves or pot-holders	6. ATS, CRH
7. Dowel stick	
8. Dye	8. BAC, BG, DTC, EH, F, JLH, MAC, SAC, TAC, WCC
9. Rubber bands	
10. Yardage strips	
11. Carpet thread	
12. Needle	
13. Clothespins (spring type)	
14. Yardage	

*Letters refer to mail order outlets listed in *Appendix B: Addresses of Suppliers.*

1   Prepare the fabric by washing it in soapy water and rinsing it in clear water to remove the sizing from the fabric. REASON: Sizing in the fabric will prevent the dye from "locking into" the fibers.

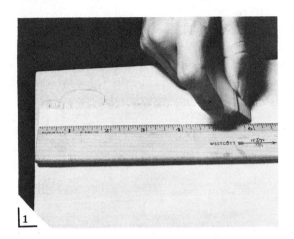 

2   Using a ruler, mark the fabric at 2-inch intervals across the width of the fabric from selvage to selvage. Do this at the top edge, middle, and bottom edge of the fabric.

 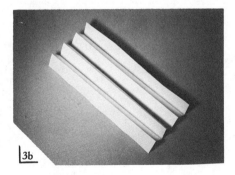

3   Fold the fabric all the way down its length one 2-inch width at a time. Use spring clothes pins to hold the folded fabric in place while folding. Accordian-pleat the fabric, working from one end to the other fold by fold. The folded piece of paper on the right is an example of the accordian pleat that you are folding. NOTE: It takes approximately 2 hours to fold 3 yards of 45-inch fabric.

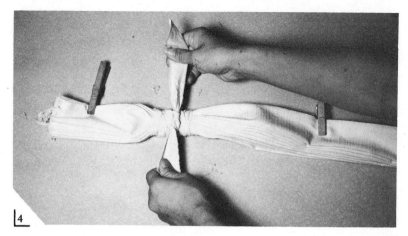

4 Cut strips of muslin approximately 2 inches wide by 36 inches long. Wrap the muslin strip around the folded fabric several times in the area where you wish to prevent the dye from entering. Space ties evenly to allow for easy matching of bands of color when sewing the fabric. In the illustration, the muslin ties were placed a hand span apart on the fabric. Tie the muslin strips with a double knot to prevent them from unraveling during the dyeing process. You will get better results if the area tied is narrow and the piece is not wrapped too tightly. This will allow the dye to slightly penetrate the tied areas, which will create jagged patterns that are quite beautiful because of the delicate shadings of dye.

Dyeing the Fabric

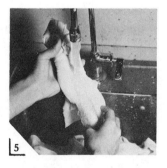

5 Prepare the dye according to the directions on the dye package. Soak the fabric thoroughly with water. This will help pull the dye into the fabric. Put the fabric into the dye pot and follow the directions for dyeing on the dye package. When the dyeing is completed, put on rubber gloves and rinse the fabric thoroughly to remove any loose dye. (Using rubber gloves prevents your hands from being dyed.)

6   Dry the fabric and remove the muslin ties. Unfold and iron the fabric. Sew the fabric into its final form.

SEWN TIE DYE

In making a sewn tie dye piece, carpet thread or a medium weight crochet cotton is the best type of thread to use. The thread must be strong so that it will not break when the fabric is gathered on it and when the thread is tied tightly. A hand-sewn running stitch will not work in this process because it does not allow the fabric to be gathered tightly enough together to prevent the dye from entering the fabric. In order to achieve a more solid line, a hand-sewn zigzag stitch, shown in step 1, is used. Designs used in sewn tie dye are usually simple, large, and bold rather than detailed, small, and delicate. For example, fabric may be folded in half and then half a heart sewn on the fold. Rectangles and squares may be sewn and the inside of the design tied up with the excess thread. In sewn tie dye it is better to complete the sewing before you gather the fabric along the thread and tie the thread. REASON: This allows you to see where to do your sewing, especially if you decide not to draw your pattern first. In the process below, the fabric was originally yellow, so where thread was sewn remained yellow and the fabric was then dyed green. In the second part of this process, the sewn line retained both the yellow and the green lines when the dye was discharged, or the fabric bleached. Bleaching the fabric turned it a light beige, so that the sewn lines were green and yellow against the light beige. You may decide to start with white fabric and sew a white line and dye your fabric blue; or you may decide to start with a navy blue fabric and sew a navy blue line and bleach your fabric, which will produce a dark line against a light background.

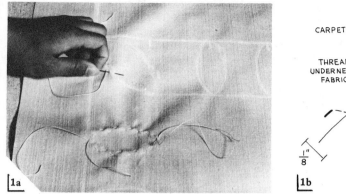

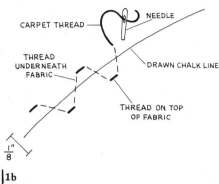

CARPET THREAD

NEEDLE

THREAD
UNDERNEATH
FABRIC

DRAWN CHALK LINE

THREAD ON TOP
OF FABRIC

$\frac{1}{8}''$

1a

1b

1   Wash the fabric to remove the sizing. With chalk, sketch out the plan for sewing. This should be done on the back side of the fabric because sometimes the chalk does not come out after dyeing. Sew across the chalk lines in a zigzag fashion as shown in the drawing on the right. Sew each line with a separate thread, leaving a few inches of thread at the beginning and end of each sewn line so that it can be easily pulled and tied. All sewing should be completed before any of the strings are pulled. REASON: It is much easier to follow your design and to see what your design is if you do this.

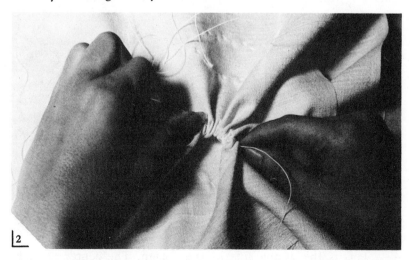

2

2   Pull each thread separately to gather the fabric. Tie the ends of each thread tightly in a double knot.

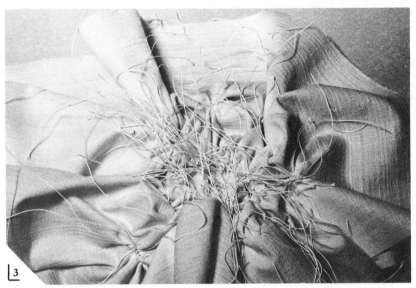

3   This is what the right side of your piece will look like when you have finished the tying. Do not cut the threads, because there is less chance of the threads coming untied if they remain long. The ends are also easier to find if they are not cut.

4   This is the wrong side of the design. The center of each design becomes a puff of fabric. This may be tied if you wish to block out some of the dye in the center of the design.

Dyeing the Fabric

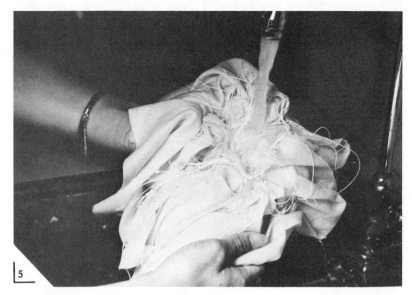

5   Prepare the dye according to the directions on the package. Wet the fabric thoroughly to help pull the dye into the fabric. Put your fabric into the dye and dye it according to the directions on the dye package. When the dyeing is finished, rinse the fabric thoroughly to remove any loose dye. Wear rubber gloves while you work.

Preparing the Fabric for Bleaching

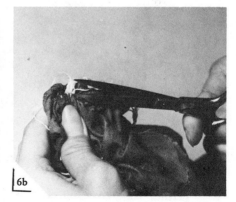

6   Carefully cut the tied threads apart. The photograph on the right shows the design after the first dyeing.

7   Following the original design, sew with a zigzag stitch on both sides of the originally sewn line.

8   Gather the fabric on each set of threads on both sides of the original design. NOTE: An additional line was sewn up the center of each leaf design.

9   Tie each set of threads with a double knot.

Bleaching the Fabric

10   Measure half a cup of bleach and pour it into simmering water. Next, wet the fabric thoroughly, and then place it into the bleach for about 3 to 5 minutes. Using pot holders or asbestos gloves, carry the pot to the sink. Turn on the cold water and allow it to cool the fabric, water, and pot. Rinse the fabric thoroughly.

Finishing the Project

11   When it is dry, carefully cut the sewn threads from the fabric and iron it. The finished project illustrated here is a decorator pillow.

Various tie dye methods can be combined in one piece. At the hem of a long skirt large circles can be created by pulling the fabric into cones and tying the base of the cones with twine. Above and below the area of the circles scallops could be sewn and the fabric gathered and tied. If you are doing this, it would be easier to sew the scallops first and then locate the areas where you wanted the circles; otherwise, the scallops could be uneven.

If you would like to create a tie dyed area only around the neck and hemline of a dress you plan to sew, cut out the various pattern pieces and tie and dye them before sewing the dress together. The reason for this is that sometimes the facings or hems of a finished dress will take the dye unevenly and show an unfavorable dye distribution.

Another idea would be to tie and bleach certain areas and then before untying those areas, dye the piece another color. After removing the ties or twine, sew a double line pattern across the two differently colored areas, gather the fabric, tie the thread, and then bleach the fabric again. This would leave a multicolored line on a light background. A little experimenting could open up a whole new world in this medium.

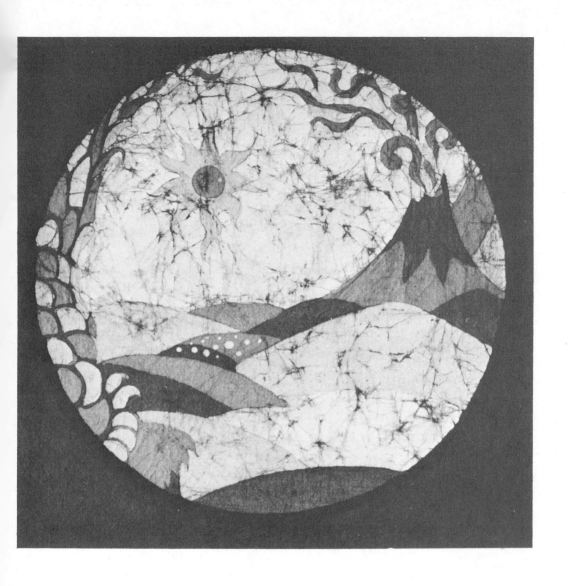

four

BATIK

"Circular Fantasy" by Marquis Miyauchi is an imaginative batik showing a natural crackle effect.

Batik is a method of dye resist in which wax is used to prevent the dye from entering the fabric in the waxed areas. True batiks consist of images made by small dots of wax. The "crackle effect" usually identifies a batik. This effect, usually the last step in making a batik, can be achieved by covering the entire batik with wax and when the wax has hardened, it is cracked; this allows the dye (usually the darkest color in a batik) to seep into the cracks, creating a textured background on the batik. The crackle effect is shown in "Circular Fantasy" by Marquis Miyauchi and "Together-Altogether" by Jerome Wallace.

PROJECTS

Batik patterns on sarongs were originally used in Java to distinguish certain classes of people from others; only certain classes were permitted to make and wear particular patterns. Batik was usually done on a fabric to be used for clothing; today, however, there are many other possibilities for batiks.

"Together—Altogether" by Jerome Wallace is a batik done using natural dyes that the artist has made from roots, lichens, leaves, and other plant materials. The crackle effect was carefully planned by using a bird's quill to remove wax in straight lines.

They can be used for wall hangings, lamp shades, purses, bedspreads, table runners, tablecloths, and curtains. Batiks can be created on heavy weight parchment paper as well as cloth. Batiks may be suspended from a rod, stretched on stretcher bars and framed with strips of wood, placed between two pieces of glass and put in front of a window, imbedded in plastic resin, or stretched over a light box with fluorescent tubes behind it.

Gary Iseri proudly wears his batik Aloha shirt.

METHODS

Although there are several methods of dye resist (tying, sewing, paste mixtures of cornstarch or flour, polyester resin, and waxes), two traditional methods of waxing and dyeing batiks are given below.

In the first method, batik wax (one part paraffin and four parts beeswax) is put on the area that is not to be dyed, and the fabric is dyed the lightest of the dye colors that are to be used. Wax is then added to the areas that are to be kept the first dye color, and the fabric is dyed with a medium color dye. Wax is then placed over the area that is to be kept the medium color. The piece is finally placed in the darkest dye color. The wax is removed by ironing and boiling or by dry cleaning. This is the easiest of the two basic methods, and is the one that will be used in this chapter.

The second method involves waxing out all of the areas except the one area that is to be dyed. After the fabric has been dyed, the wax is removed. New wax is placed over all the areas that will not be dyed the second color. Areas that are to be a combination of the first and second color are not waxed either. After the fabric has been dyed the second color, the wax is again removed. New wax is then placed over all the areas that will not be dyed the third color; areas that will be combined with the third color to make other colors are not waxed. After the third dyeing, all the wax is removed. This process is continued until all the desired colors have been applied.

The advantage of the second method is that it can produce clear yellows, reds, and blues; whereas in the first method the colors are muted because they are built up on top of each other. In the first method, if you were to put blue on top of yellow, you would not have a clear blue, you would have green. The effect you want to produce will determine what method you use.

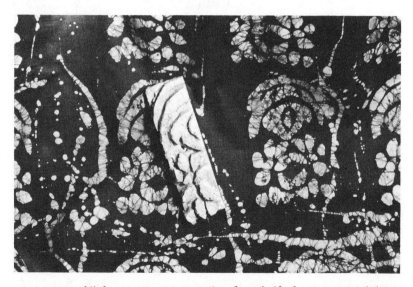

A sponge refill for a mop was carved to form half of a symmetrical design by Loretta Hicks. After dipping it in hot wax and stamping one half of the design on one side of the fabric, the fabric was turned over and stamped on the other side to complete the symmetrical design. To break the rigidity of the design, wax was dribbled between the stamped designs.

SUPPLIES

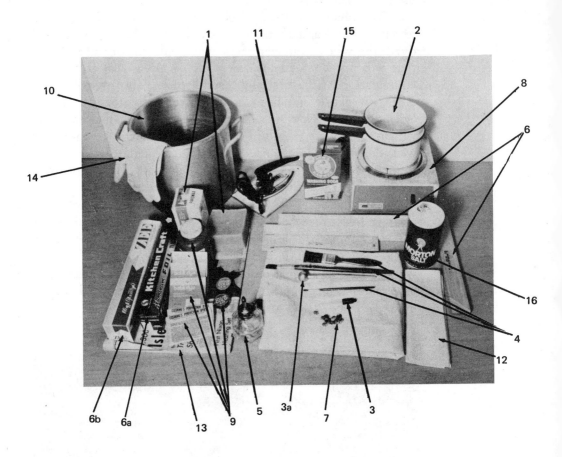

PRECAUTIONS

Paraffin is highly flammable. Paraffin or any wax should be heated in a double boiler with the wax in the top half and the water in the lower half to keep the wax from burning. The wax should be melted on an electric stove or electric burner because there will be less chance of the wax igniting than if a gas burner is used. In applying the hot wax to the fabric you will be using

Supplies	Sources of Supplies*
1. Batik wax or paraffin and beeswax	1. BAC, BG, CCI, EH, MAC, SAC, TAC
2. Double boiler	
3. Eyedropper or	
3A. Tjanting tool	3A. BAC, BG, CCI, EH, MAC, SAC, TAC
4. Paint brushes	
5. Alcohol lamp	5. ATS, BAC, BG, CCI, CRH, EH, JLH, SAC, SI, TAC
6. Stretcher bars or	
6A. Aluminum foil or	
6B. Wax paper	
7. Thumb tacks	
8. Electric stove or burner	
9. Cold water dyes	9. BAC, BG, CCI, DTC, EH, F, JLH, MAC, SAC, TAC, WCC
10. Dye pot	
11. Iron	
12. Paper towels	
13. Newspapers	
14. Rubber gloves	
15. Washing soda (if not included in dye package)	
16. Salt	

*Letters refer to mail order outlets listed in *Appendix B: Addresses of Suppliers.*

an eye dropper or tjanting tool, which will have to be heated in the flame of an alcohol lamp or candle to melt the hardened wax. The area of exposed wax is small and will burn out before any damage is caused, but always be careful when heating the eyedropper or tjanting tool.

DYES

Natural dyes can be used cold and set with a mordant (a fixitive substance). Cold water dyes (fiber reactive dyes) are usually used in batik work because if hot water dyes were used, the wax on the fabric would melt. There are many types of cold water dyes on the market: Batikit, Fibrec, Inko, Procion. Inko dye requires heat to bring out the color; when the wax is ironed out of the fabric, the heat from the iron will set the Inko dye. Another possibility is liquid acrylic paint, which is very permanent and can be brushed on in the desired areas; however, it is necessary to put wax around the areas where the paint is to be applied or the paint will bleed into undesired areas. The wax acts as a "stop" for the paint.

FABRIC

Cotton or silk is usually used for batik work. Before you begin, you should always test the dye you are using to be sure it will work with the fabric that you have chosen. Synthetic fibers do not accept dye fully, but polyester fabric can be colored with a solution of acrylic paint that will be permanent. Light weight fabrics are best to use for batik work because it is easy for the wax to penetrate through the fabric. Since the wax will not penetrate through heavy weight fabric, both sides need to be waxed.

CRACKLE EFFECT

In order to achieve the "crackle effect" in batik, the entire piece should be waxed. Bend the waxed piece back on itself to create cracks in the wax. The cracks may be done casually or they may be planned. You can achieve a spider web effect by cracking the fabric in a radial pattern. Make horizontal or vertical cracks by gathering the fabric in an accordian pleat in the direction you want the cracks. You can create lines by using a blunt instrument such as a bird's quill to remove wax in the desired places. The wax must be removed from both the front and back sides of the fabric or the dye will not penetrate it. Use of a sharp instrument may weaken or tear the fabric.

PROCEDURE

Preparing the Fabric and the Wax

1   Wash the fabric to remove all sizing from the material. Dry it and iron it if you wish, but ironing is not necessary. Stretch the fabric over a frame or stretcher bars, or place it on aluminum foil or wax paper. If you stretch the fabric over a frame or stretcher bars, begin by placing the first tack in the center of the longest side of the frame and then repeat this on the opposite side. Next, place the third tack in the center of the shortest side and then on the opposite side. This creates an equal tension. Continue by dividing each area in half from the last tack to the end of the frame. Work from one side to the opposite side, back and forth to keep the tension equal. Stretch the fabric tighter by placing wedges in the corners of the stretcher bars.

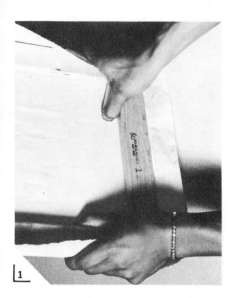 

2   Use a proportion of one part beeswax to four parts of paraffin. This allows the wax to retain its liquid state longer and also permits the crackle effect to occur. You can speed up the melting process by breaking up the wax into small pieces. Put the wax into the top part of a double boiler with water in the bottom part. Wax is flammable and should not be placed directly on a burner. Because of the high flammability of wax, it is safer to use an electric burner than a gas burner.

Creating the Design

3   Sketch a design heavily on paper and place it beneath the material, or cut out a design and place it on top of the material, or create a stamp with which to apply the wax to the fabric—a sponge or wooden form can be used for a stamp. If you use metal for a stamp, keep it warm so the wax will not harden on it; if you let it get too hot, it will scorch the fabric.

Applying the Wax

4   Apply the wax to the fabric using either a tjanting tool, eyedropper, brush, or a stamp. Apply the wax quickly so that it penetrates through to the back of the fabric. If the wax does

not penetrate the fabric, it looks white on the top and you will not be able to see the design on the back side. You will have to put wax on the back side of the fabric if it has not penetrated through; otherwise, the dye will penetrate the fabric from the back side.

5   Keep the wax liquid in the eyedropper or tjanting tool by holding it over a candle flame or the flame of an alcohol lamp. To prevent the wax from dripping out of the spout of the tjanting tool, hold a cotton ball or a small wad of fabric under the spout when carrying it over the fabric.

Completing the Project

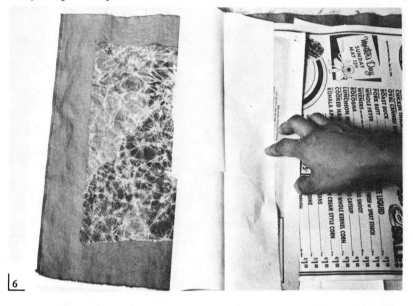

6   Using either cold water dyes or acrylic paint, dye or paint the fabric. Wet the fabric before placing it into the dye so that the dye will be pulled evenly into the fabric. Wear rubber gloves while dyeing the fabric to avoid dyeing your hands. Do not put the fabric into a dryer to dry it, because this will melt the wax. Iron the wax out of the fabric by placing it between layers of newspaper and paper toweling. Place the paper toweling between the fabric and the newspaper to prevent the newsprint from transferring to the fabric. There should be a layer of paper toweling next to the fabric and about five sheets of newspaper under the fabric. On top of the fabric there

should be one layer of paper toweling and one sheet of newspaper on top of that. As the wax melts through the top sheet of newspaper, place another sheet of newspaper on top of the waxed newspaper. Continue adding a layer of newspaper as each layer is waxed. Do not remove the waxed newspaper. When no wax or very little wax comes through the newspaper, you are finished. To remove any remaining wax in the fabric, repeat the ironing process with fresh newspaper and toweling, dry clean it, or boil it in water.

7   Repeat steps 4 through 6 for each color you want to use until you have completed your batik. The wax does not need to be removed after each dye color has been applied unless you wish to do so. Frame or sew the batik into its final form.

FURTHER SUGGESTIONS

Scraps of "left over" batiks can be sewn together to create patchwork batik edges on sleeves, hems, legs of jeans, tablecloths, or bedspreads. Batik dresses can be carefully planned by cutting out the dress first, and then creating the batik design around necklines or down one side of a long dress or around the hemline. Batiks can be "encrusted" with embroidery or overlaid with various colored transparent fabrics. More possibilities can be explored if you combine batik with silk screening, stenciling, block printing, or tie dye.

five

STITCHERY

"Moonwalk" by the author shows a use of the reverse appliqué technique in which the "top" fabric has been cut open to reveal the fabric beneath, which shows the sun and the earth. The large appliqué in brown on top of this represents the astronauts.

Stitchery is a creative exploration of color and texture that utilizes yarn, string, twine, thread, and woven and nonwoven fabric. In a way, it resembles mosaic work in that many small things are put together to make up the whole. You can experiment with a variety of yarns and threads whose textures vary from shiny metallic threads to soft mohair and lumpy bouclé yarns. Stitchery gives you an adventure in color from yarns through fabrics. The basic idea behind making a stitchery piece is to gather together materials, colors, and textures that seem to work together. Look for fabrics whose colors and textures work with the yarns you have chosen. Try not to be inhibited by the fact that some yarns could never possibly fit through the eye of a needle because of their thickness; these yarns can be attached in other ways, as you will see in this chapter.

This halter created and modeled by Brenda Ha shows the combined use of macramé and the "tight approach" in stitchery.

GETTING IT TOGETHER

The easiest way to begin to gather the fabrics and yarns you wish to use in your stitchery is to find one color with the texture that you like and want to use in your finished panel. This might be a piece of turquoise velveteen fabric or a few strands of soft pink mohair yarn. You might want to make your beginning pieces stand out, in which case you could seek a color and texture that would contrast with what you have. For example, the turquoise velveteen might be beautifully set off by a rust brown piece of burlap or shiny silver metallic threads. If you want the whole piece to blend together, you might seek

This panel created by Kathleen Miyamura shows the "loose approach" to stitchery.

Created by the Cuna Indians, this mola *shows the use of a reverse appliqué in which openings are cut in the top piece of cloth to allow the color beneath to show. Additional colors are also appliquéd both on top of and underneath the "top" piece of fabric. Molas are decorative pieces usually found on the bodice section of dresses worn by the Cuna Indians.*

colors that are next to turquoise on the color wheel. At the same time you are looking for similar colors you could be seeking contrasting textures that would add visual interest to the colors you choose. For example, if you chose the turquoise velveteen, you might try to find a homespun or rough weave of light turquoise and contrast that with a crepe or the flat surface finish of a piece of broadcloth in a medium turquoise color. When you have a concentration of fabric texture, you would probably want to keep the yarn texture subdued. In another stitchery piece you might decide to concentrate on using a variety of yarn and thread textures. Think of stitchery as a method of changing the surface on which you work by encrusting it with a variety of textures.

APPLIQUÉ

Appliqué is the method of attaching one piece of fabric to another larger piece of fabric. In the "loose approach" to stitchery, a simple Running Stitch or Blanket Stitch can be used to apply a piece of fabric to a larger piece of fabric. There is no attempt to turn under the edges of the fabric before doing the stitches.

Running Stitch*   Blanket Stitch*

In the "tight approach" to stitchery, appliqué work can be done using the Blind Stitch or the Overcast Stitch by hand or the machine Zigzag Stitch. In the Blind Stitch or Overcast Stitch, the fabric edges are clipped and folded under before they are stitched. In the Blind Stitch the thread rides along the inside of the folded edge and comes out only to pick up one thread from the bottom fabric and return under the folded edge

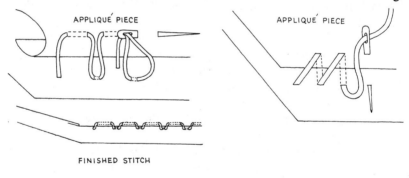

APPLIQUÉ PIECE   APPLIQUÉ PIECE

FINISHED STITCH

Blind Stitch   Overcast Stitch

in nearly the same location from which it emerged. The idea is to have a stitch that does not show. In the Overcast Stitch, the thread rides along under the bottom fabric and comes up to catch a thread from the folded appliqué edge and returns under the bottom fabric close to the same spot it emerged from. In using the Zigzag Stitch on the sewing machine, the fabric that is to be appliquéd is pinned to the bottom piece of fabric. The edges are not turned under. The appliqué is first attached to the

*SOURCE: *One Hundred Embroidery Stitches* (New York: Coats and Clark, Inc.).

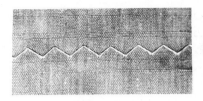

*Basting Zigzag Stitch
done on the sewing machine*

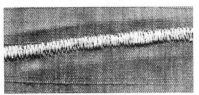

*Tight Zigzag Stitch done
on top of the Basting
Zigzag Stitch*

larger piece with a wide Basting Zigzag Stitch; then a tight Zigzag Stitch is used over the first stitching. The Basting Zigzag keeps the fabric from "crawling" when the tighter Zigzag Stitch is used.

EMBROIDERY STITCHES

Chain Stitch

There are three stitches that are basic to stitchery work: the Chain Stitch, the Couching Stitch, and the French Knot. To do the Chain Stitch:

1. Bring the needle up through the fabric.
2. Make a loop with the yarn, holding it down with your thumb, and return the needle to the point where the yarn emerged from the fabric.
3. Bring the needle back up through the fabric about $\frac{1}{8}$ inch in front of the previous stitch.
4. Pull the needle out on top of the loop just formed.
5. Make a new loop and follow steps 2, 3, and 4 to continue the Chain Stitch.

Chain Stitch*

Couching Stitch

The Couching Stitch is used to secure thick yarns to the backing. It can also be used decoratively. For the Couching Stitch bring the thread up through the fabric, over the yarn, and back down through the fabric. Carry the thread under the fabric until you bring it through again to go over the yarn and take it

*SOURCE: *One Hundred Embroidery Stitches* (New York: Coats and Clark, Inc.).

back down through the fabric. For decorative use, a contrasting color may be used and two stitches placed next to each other, or a Cross Stitch can be made over the larger yarn with the couching thread. Other possible variations may occur to you as you do this stitch. You can be very inventive with stitchery. It is not necessary to follow well-known stitches; you can create your own stitches and methods of doing them. Stitches can often be created by wrapping or weaving or sewing other threads around those that you have already placed on the stitchery surface. Here the idea of encrusting a surface comes to the fore.

Couching Stitch*

Weaving other threads
around a stitch

French Knot

French Knot*

The third stitch that is greatly used in stitchery work is the French Knot. Bring the needle up through the fabric at the point where the knot is to be made, and wrap the thread two or three times around the point of the needle. Insert the needle in the fabric as close as possible to the spot where the thread emerges. Pull the needle through to the back side of the fabric to form the knot. You can vary the size of the knot by varying the thickness of the thread or yarn. You can create a different knot by wrapping the thread around the needle about seven times before putting the needle back into the fabric a little further away from the original point.

There are many other very useful stitches that you can use for stitchery. *One Hundred Embroidery Stitches*, a small paperback put out by Coats and Clark, is an excellent guide. In working with this little book, you will find that new stitches will develop from those shown, and some stitches will work well in combination with others—for example, the Cable Chain Stitch with a French Knot in the center.

*SOURCE: *One Hundred Embroidery Stitches* (New York: Coats and Clark, Inc.).

SUPPLIES

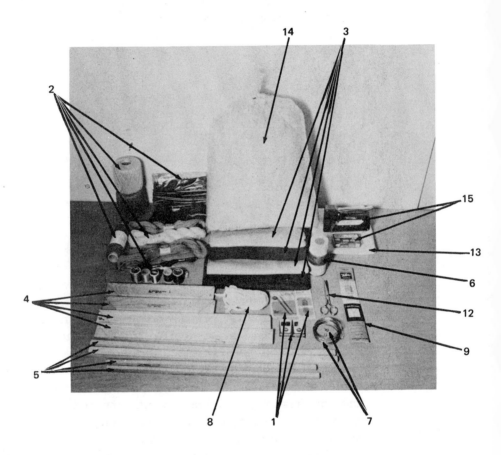

Supplies	Sources of Supplies*
1. Variety of needles 2. Yarns, thread, twine, etc. 3. Fabrics 4. Stretcher bars for wall hanging 5. Strips of wood for wall hanging 6. Stain or spray paint for wall hanging 7. Screw eyes and picture wire for wall hanging 8. ¼ inch wide cotton cording for pillow 9. Zipper for pillow 10. Sewing machine for pillow (not shown) 11. Zipper foot for sewing machine for pillow (not shown) 12. Scissors 13. Muslin for pillow 14. Kapok for pillow 15. Staple gun and staples for wall hanging	Except for stretcher bars, which can be purchased from art supply stores, and wood, stain, spray paint, screw eyes, and picture wire, which can be purchased from building supply houses, most of the other supplies can be obtained from yarn and yardage departments and stores.

*Letters refer to mail order outlets listed in *Appendix B: Addresses of Suppliers.*

Preparing the Materials

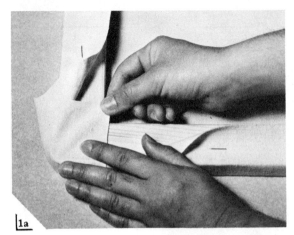

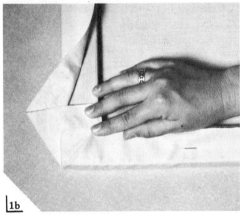

1   Gather fabric and yarns that are compatible and yet offer variation in either color or texture. Select a heavy weight fabric for the background fabric. A close weave would be preferable. Fabric for the background should not be so thick that it is difficult to put a needle through it. Stretcher bars can be used for the base on which to work and can then be used to display your completed piece. Assembling the stretcher bars is easy. Stretch the background fabric over the stretcher bars. Working from the center on opposite sides, staple the fabric to the back of the stretcher bars. Miter the corners by first folding a right angle on the corner. Bring the sides over on top of the square formed at the corner. Staple across the mitered corner.

Attaching the Materials

2

2   Arrange fabrics and yarns over the surface until you have achieved a pleasing arrangement and balance. Baste fabrics down in the desired position using a Running Stitch. Remove this basting thread later when the fabrics have been secured permanently.

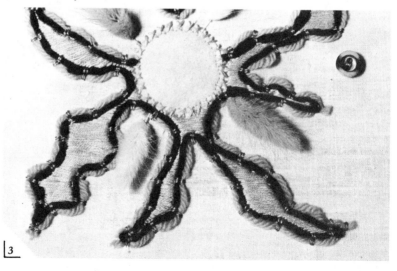

3

3   Use the Blanket Stitch, Running Stitch, or Cross Stitch to attach the fabrics. Select contrasting yarns and threads to make these stitches. Attach other 'yarns to the surface by Couching if the yarn is thick, or use some of the stitches mentioned earlier.

Completing the Panel

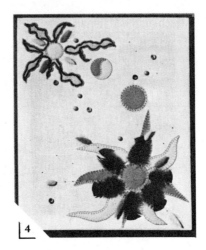

4   After your panel has been completed, stain or spray paint strips of wood a contrasting or coordinating color. Using small brads, nail the strips of wood to the stretcher bars. Secure screw eyes and picture wire to the back of the frame.

TIGHT TECHNIQUE: MAKING A STITCHERY PILLOW

Planning and Preparing the Design

1   Decide on the size of the pillow. Draw an outline of the pillow on a piece of wrapping paper. This will give you the working area for your design. Create a design. You can make thumbnail sketches and then select the best one to be enlarged. You can develop designs from natural forms, flowers, fruits, or primitive designs of the Incas, Aztecs, and Mayans.

2   To enlarge your design, draw a grid over it. Let each square represent 1 inch of the final enlarged piece. For example, in your small sketch, you might make the squares ¼ inch apart, and then in the enlarged piece have the squares 1 inch apart. Copy your design square-by-square.

Preparing the Appliqué Piece

3   Cut out from your paper design the pieces that are to be appliquéd. (It is a good idea to make a second copy of your design that you can follow later.) Pin these paper patterns to the fabric you are using for the appliqués. Sew a Running Stitch in a contrasting color around the paper pattern pieces. This is so

you will know where to fold your fabric under for the Blind Stitch. Remove the paper patterns and cut out the fabric leaving about a ½-inch margin outside of the Running Stitch; this extra material will be folded under later.

4   Clip the curved edges of the design.

5   Baste the appliqué to the background fabric that you have cut out to the desired size and shape. If the appliqué is narrow, fold under the edges and baste down along the edges. If the appliqué is wide, turn the edges down later when doing the Blind Stitch.

6

6   Using a thread the same color as the appliqué, begin the Blind Stitch by placing the knot at the end of the thread in the folded section of the appliqué. Pick up one thread from the bottom fabric and go back into the area near where the needle emerged the first time. Continue this procedure until the appliqué has been attached.

7

7   Embellish the surface of the appliqué and the area surrounding it with a variety of yarns and stitches.

8   Cut a 2-inch velveteen or cotton broadcloth strip on the bias. Fold the bias strip over ¼-inch cotton cording.

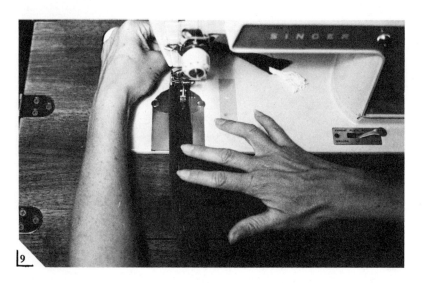

9   Using a zipper foot attachment on the sewing machine, sew the strip close to the cording.

10 Baste the corded fabric to the outer edge of the surface of the embellished side of the stitchery as shown here. This creates a "finished" edge to the pillow.

11 Cut one piece of cloth about three-fourths the length of the pillow, having the same width as the pillow (bottom piece). Cut a second piece the width of the pillow and about one-fourth the length of the pillow (top piece). This piece should overlap the bottom piece by 2 inches.

12

12 With the right sides facing each other, sew the top and bottom pieces together using the Basting Stitch on the sewing machine; however, sew a tighter stitch on the two outer ends. This seam should be about 1 to 2 inches in from the edge.

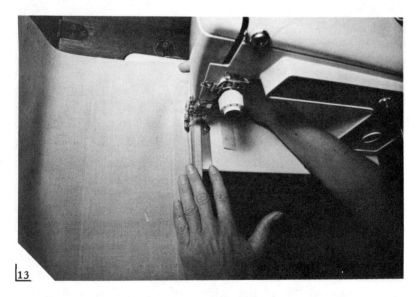

13

13 Following the directions on the zipper package, sew the zipper to the bottom section near the seam line.

62 STITCHERY

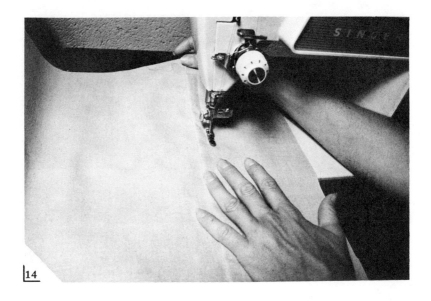

14   Turn the pillow back right side facing up and, following the directions on the zipper package, sew the overlapping section of the cloth on the top section of the pillow back.

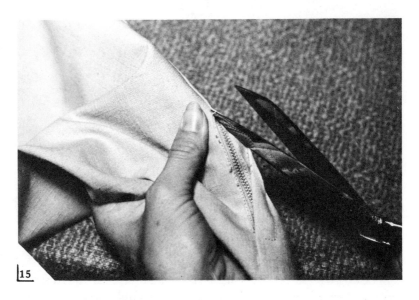

15   Remove the basting thread to open the basted seam of the zipper. Open the zipper.

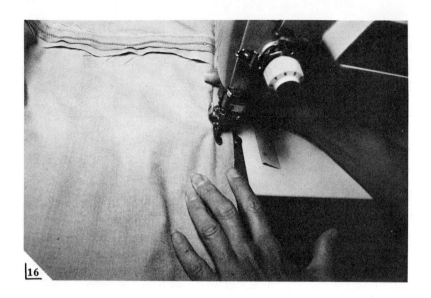

16 With the right sides together, baste the front and back pieces together. Using the zipper foot, sew the two pieces together close to the edge of the basted cording. Turn the pillow right side out through the zipper opening.

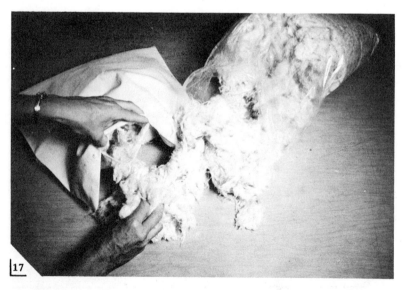

17 Cut two pieces of muslin the same size as the finished pillow. Sew a ½-inch seam all the way around these two pieces leaving a 7-inch opening on one side. Turn the muslin bag right side out and stuff it with kapok.

18

18 Sew up the opening on the sewing machine or by hand using the Blind Stitch. Place the muslin bag with the kapok in it inside the pillow. Close the zipper and the pillow is finished.

FURTHER SUGGESTIONS

Stitchery work on surfaces that will receive a lot of wear and tear should be done in the "tight technique," whereas stitchery on surfaces that are just decorative may be done in the "loose technique." Children enjoy clothing that has stitchery work on it: kittens, clowns, gingerbread men, little people holding balloons. Stitchery work lends itself to clothing decoration and can be very sophisticated when done with fine fabrics such as velveteens and satins. Kitchen curtains can become very gay and cheerful when stitchery is applied to them. Stitchery can also be attached to embroidery hoops—large and small. The outer hoop becomes a frame for the stitchery panel. Washable fabrics should be preshrunk by washing before they are used in stitchery work, especially if the final product is to go into the washing machine for cleaning. Nonwashable wools, rayons, satins, silks, and similar fabrics should be drycleaned before use.

six

TEXTILE SILK SCREENING

On the preceding page, three different screens were used for the different colors in this transparent voile fabric printed by Carole Langner. Beautiful depth can be achieved by the overlaying of this printed voile as is shown here.

Silk screening is a quick and simple method of stenciling multiple images on paper, cardboard, plastics, or fabric.* With a silk screen and textile inks you can decorate T-shirts, pillow cases, and a variety of fabrics from soft cotton velvets to shiny silks. When purchasing textile ink, find out what types of fabric it will print best on. Fabrics with crease-resistant finishes do not absorb the textile inks very well. Purchase your supplies from someone who can supply you with both the textile inks and the necessary materials to block out the inks; otherwise, you could dissolve your stencil while you are printing your fabric.

To do silk screening, an open frame on which silk or other fine-meshed fabric is stretched is used to hold the image that is to be stenciled. This image may be painted on the screen with liquids, such as glue or tusche, or it may be blocked out by adhering a paper or lacquer stencil to the screen. After the image has been attached to the screen, ink is forced through the screen with a squeegee. The ink goes through the screen and onto the cloth beneath except in the areas that have been blocked out on the screen. When many different colors are used in one design, a screen must be prepared for each color. These screens need to be keyed or registered so that the colors are

Jo Ann Lum models her first silk screened shirt. It was created using only one screen.

In this halter and hot pants set by Denise Go, the fabric pieces were cut out first so that the stenciled design could be placed on the flat fabric where it was desired.

*Silk is being replaced by other fabrics, such as polyester, so silk is not always used for a screen in this process; however, because so many artists and craftsmen still use the term "silk screening" it has been used throughout this chapter with the above reservation in mind.

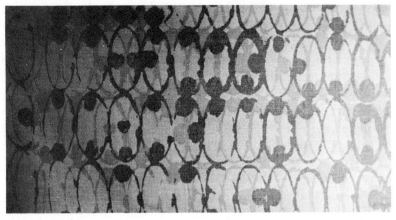

A part of a silk screened fabric by Carole Langner showing the same screen used twice. In the second printing the screen was moved over slightly and a different color ink was used.

printed in the correct location on the fabric. When printing on a piece of fabric that has already been sewn, registration can be "eyeballed" through the transparent stencil film. When printing an overall design on yardage, however, a printing table and a crossbar must be used for the registration of the design. Each screen for the multiple color process must have registration marks on it so that the colors will be correctly aligned. First, all the screens must be keyed to the design; then the screens must be keyed or registered on the cross bar of the printing table. To be certain that the screens are keyed to the design; (1) mark a small cross at the middle of the top, bottom, and side edges of your design; (2) tape your design on a piece of paper larger than the outside edge of the frame of your screen; (3) draw an outline on the paper of the outside edge of the frame of your screen. All screens for each of the colors used should be located within this outlined area when each color for the design is blocked out with liquids or the stencil is adhered to the screen. The position for the screens during printing can be marked on the crossbar and on the screen with registration marks.

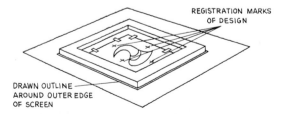

REGISTRATION MARKS OF DESIGN

DRAWN OUTLINE AROUND OUTER EDGE OF SCREEN

Registration marks for keying a design on a screen.

Allowance should be made for parts of the screen that will overlap so that the edges of the design meet, so it is better to have the registration mark in the center of the side of the screen rather than at the ends of the screen. The drawing below shows these registration marks on the screen and crossbar and indicates the next position of the screen with dotted lines.

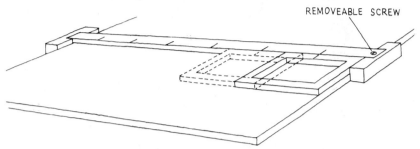

Printing table for multiple screenings.

A printing table for the registration of overall designs on yardage should be approximately 5 feet wide by 16 feet long so that the entire fabric can be laid out flat on the table and pinned down during the printing process. Thick felt and a layer of muslin or several layers of felt and a layer of muslin should be stapled to the bottom edge of the printing table as shown in the drawing.

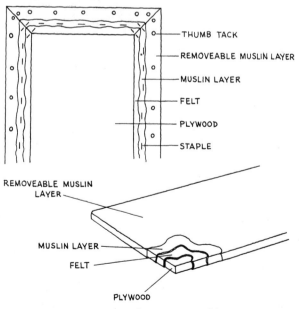

Covering for printing table.

SUPPLIES

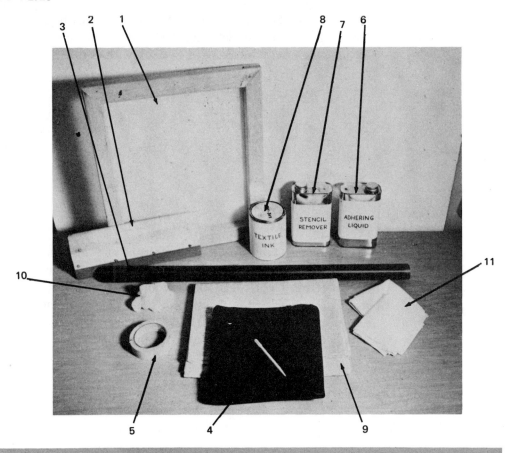

The printing table may be ¾-inch plywood that is placed on three or four sawhorses so that it can be easily disassembled, or it may be of the more permanent variety with a lip along the edge and a storage space for screens below it. An additional layer of muslin should be tacked to the table around the bottom edges. This backing piece of muslin should be removed and washed after each printing session because the dye from the printing will seep through the fabric that is being printed and may transfer to the next fabric that is printed on the table. The crossbar that the printing screens are placed against to keep the printed design parallel throughout the printing process may be made of pine approximately 2 to 3 inches thick by 6 inches

Supplies	Sources of Supplies*
1. Silk screen	Most supplies for silk screen
2. Squeegee	work can be found in art supply
3. Stencil film	stores; however, other suppliers
4. Stencil knife	of silk screen materials are listed
5. Masking tape or mask-out	in Appendix B of this book
6. Adhering liquid	under the following letters:
7. Stencil film remover or	ACC, EH, MAC, NDC, SAC,
lacquer thinner	SPS, and TAC. Further suppliers
8. Textile inks	of silk screen materials may be
9. Newspapers	found by consulting a local tele-
10. Cotton balls	phone directory.
11. Rags	
12. Felt	
13. Printing table for yardage	
(not shown)	

*Letters refer to mail order outlets listed in *Appendix B: Addresses of Suppliers.*

wide and longer than the width of the printing table. A piece of wood is attached to one end of the crossbar to form a right angle. Another piece of wood is attached with a screw or bolt to the other end of the crossbar to form a right angle; this will allow the piece to be removed when moving the crossbar up to the next position on the printing table. Another possible arrangement of the crossbar would be to have it fit the width of the table exactly so that it can be clamped into position by a C-clamp on both ends. To ensure that the crossbar is parallel throughout the printing process, measure the distances on both ends of the crossbar to the end of the table when moving the crossbar from one position to the next on the printing table.

PROCEDURE

Preparing the Fabric and the Design

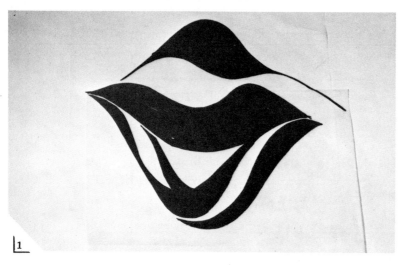

1

1   Wash the fabric or object that is to be silk screened. This is necessary to remove the sizing and/or any dirt that may prevent the textile ink from penetrating the fabric. When printing on fabric that has already been sewn, place felt or newspaper between the two pieces of fabric so that the ink does not seep through from one piece to the other. Create the design for the stencil on a piece of paper. The dark areas indicate the areas to be inked. These will be cut from the stencil so the ink can go through these areas.

2

2   Place the stencil film over the design so that the lacquer surface is on top and the backing that will be peeled off is on the bottom next to the design. NOTE: The lacquer surface is shiny.

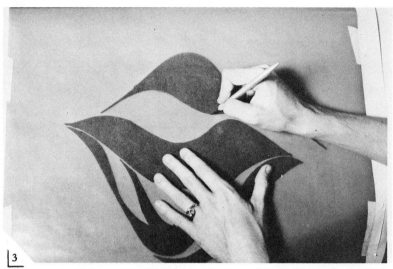

3   Position the design and tape it to the stencil film. Using a stencil knife, cut through the lacquer layer but not through the backing.

4   Using the point of the stencil knife, carefully lift off the area of the design that will be inked. Do not remove the stencil backing because it holds in position the lacquer areas that will block out the ink during the printing process.

5   Place the stencil, with the lacquer side facing up, underneath the silk screen so that the surface of the screen is pressed against the lacquer surface of the stencil. Dampen a piece of cotton with adhering fluid and have a dry piece of cotton ready. Wipe the screen with the dampened piece of cotton and then with the dry piece of cotton. The area you wiped with the dampened piece of cotton should have melted the lacquer surface of the stencil enough to adhere it to the screen. If too much fluid is used, it will cause the lacquer surface to disintegrate, so take care not to get the piece of cotton too wet. This area that you adhered to the screen should look slightly darker than the rest of the stencil. Continue the process of adhering the stencil to the screen by slightly overlapping the area just adhered.

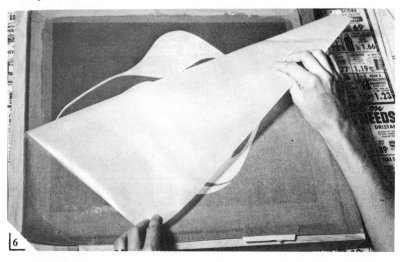

6   After the lacquer area of the design has been adhered to the screen, block out the outer edges of the design with additional stencil material, masking tape, or maskout. Allow at least fifteen minutes for the lacquer stencil to "set" and then peel off the backing paper of the lacquer stencil. The lacquer stencil now blocks out the areas that will not be printed.

Screening the Design

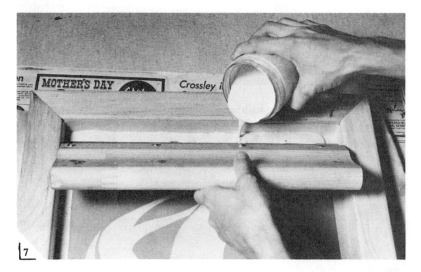

7   Dampen a piece of cloth with white vinegar and press the vinegar onto the surface that is to be printed. This will prepare the fabric to absorb the textile ink, and it will also act as a mordant to lock the ink into the fabric. Pour the ink along the end of the screen that is parallel to the squeegee.

8   With the squeegee, pull the ink across and through the screen. This can be done twice to insure a thorough penetration of the ink into the fabric. Be sure to pull all of the ink each time across the screen. It is a good idea to have someone hold the screen while you are pulling the squeegee across it so that the screen does not move. If you use textile inks that can be set by heat, such as Inko, place the printed fabric in the sun or iron

the fabric; otherwise, follow the manufacturer's directions for setting the ink. It is best not to wash the fabric that has been silk screened until about a month later to allow the ink to "set."

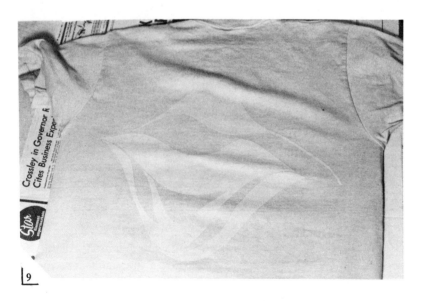

9   Photo 9 shows the first screened color. The screen was placed slightly off register on the second screening and a different color ink was used in the second screening.

Cleaning the Screen

10

10   If you are using a water based ink, wash the screen with water to remove any excess ink; otherwise, follow the manufacturer's directions for cleaning the screen. Remove any masking tape from the screen. Dampen a rag with the stencil adhering fluid or lacquer thinner. Work outside or in a well-ventilated area away from flames. Read carefully and observe all directions on the labels of these materials as they are highly flammable. Place the lacquer thinner on the stencil on the underneath part of the screen.

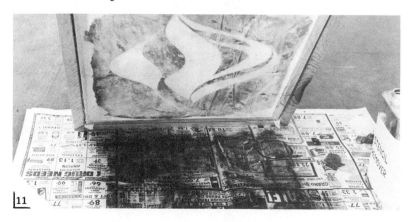

11

11   Immediately turn the screen over onto the newspapers. Soak the cloth again and dampen the surface of the screen. Lift the screen from the newspapers. The stencil will adhere to the newspapers. Repeat this process until all of the stencil has been removed from the silk screen.

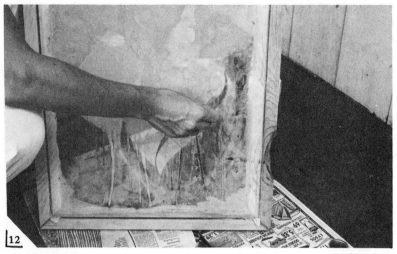

12

12 If some stencil still remains, dampen two pieces of cotton with the lacquer thinner, and with the screen standing on its side rub both sides of the screen at the same time to remove any further material.

13

13 Photo 13 shows the finished T-shirt. On the second screening two colors were used at the same time, which caused a lighter top and darker bottom on the second image.

FURTHER SUGGESTIONS

The same stencil for one color can be used again with another color—either going in another direction, or slightly off register—or it can be planned to cover part of the previously screened design, or it may be placed between the previously screened design motifs. Another possibility is to cut and flock a linoleum block and use it in conjunction with the silk screened design. Or you can tie dye the fabric first and then silk screen on top of the tie dye. In Hawaii, commercially printed fabrics are sewed inside out. This suggests the possibility of silk screening both sides of the fabric to give added depth or dimension. Sometimes, the screened design can be further embellished through the use of things such as bamboo sticks. It is not necessary to flock all objects used for printing since the texture of the surfaces of many objects, such as wood, might create desirable textures.

seven

MACRAMÉ

The chapter opening close-up of a macramé wall hanging by Naomi Beals shows the creative possibilities of macramé.

Macramé is the art of knotting twine or string to create designs similar to those in knitting and crocheting. The exact origins of this craft are uncertain; some sources say that it extends back to the thirteenth century in Arabia, others that it goes back as far as the ancient Assyrians who wore knotted fringes on their robes. The craft of macramé has been practiced by sailors who made objects that they sold in port to make a few extra coins and by women who made delicate knotted fringe and lace on napkins and altar cloths. Today this craft is enjoying a rebirth, and macramé is being used for room dividers, wall hangings, purses, jewelry, clothing, and sculptural forms. Once you learn a few basic knots, you will discover numerous possibilities for the use of macramé.

The basic knots that will be described are: Lark's Head, Square Knot, Double Half Hitch, and the Cavandoli Stitch. Following these descriptions will be a section concerning patterns and how to plan your work.

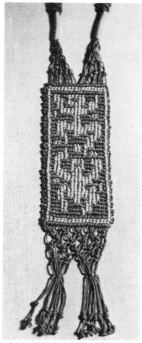

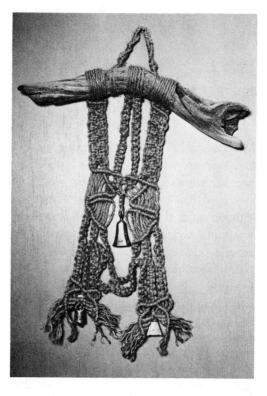

The pendant part of this macramé necklace by the author shows the use of the Cavandoli Stitch, to create petroglyph-like figures.

By using a piece of driftwood in her macramé piece, Julie Sugitan has created a rugged, primitive quality in her wall hanging.

SUPPLIES

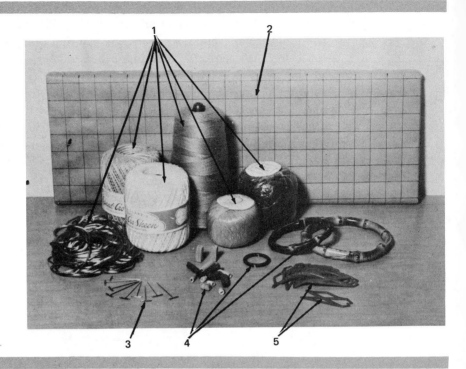

GENERAL PREPARATION

Type of Cord

Material to be used for macramé work should be tightly twisted and not too elastic. If the cord is too loosely twisted, it will become unraveled as you work with it and it will look ragged. If the cord has too much elasticity, the knots will be of uneven tension and the pattern will look and be irregular. Package wrapping twine, rattail cord, macramé cord, cotton rug yarn, acrylic and nylon yarn, as well as pearl cotton, and heavier weight crochet cotton will work well in macramé projects.

Amount of Cord Needed

For figuring how much cord or twine you will need, you must decide (1) how you will begin your piece, (2) the type of knots you will use, and (3) how close together the knots will be. In general, measure your twine to four times the finished length of the final piece. If you start with the Lark's Head Knot, your cord is folded in half, so it is measured first four times the final length and that measurement is then doubled. The cord, then,

Supplies	Sources of Supplies*
1. Twine, crochet cotton, or macramé cord	Most of the supplies for macramé can be easily found around the house. T-pins can be found in wig departments or notion departments.
2. Pillow or empty yardage bolt or corrugated cardboard	
3. T-pins	
4. Belt buckles, beads, or whatever else you wish to incorporate into your project	
5. Yarn bobbins or small rubberbands	

*Letters refer to mail order outlets listed in *Appendix B: Addresses of Suppliers.*

for a piece that begins with a Lark's Head is eight times the projected final length. If the Double Half Hitch is used frequently, as in the Cavandoli Stitch, it is better to plan your cord to be five times the finished length and then twice that if you start with the Lark's Head.

Warping the Cord

You can use a warping board to measure the length of the cord for your macramé piece. Set pegs into a board in a zigzag pattern to allow great lengths of cord to be measured in a small amount of space. Another way would be to set C-clamps with the screw end up at the beginning and end of the length of the cord desired. The lengths could then be wrapped around the C-clamps and later cut off at both ends.

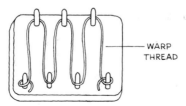

WARP THREAD

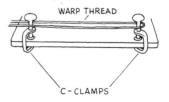

WARP THREAD

C-CLAMPS

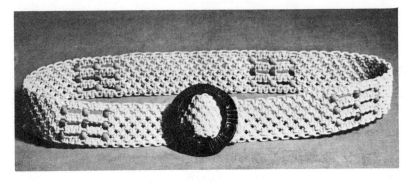

Roy Ono's belt shows the beauty of evenly knotted square knots accented by wooden beads.

Preparing the Bobbins

In order to work with macramé cords without having them get tangled, you will need to gather them up somehow. Possibilities include: (1) wrapping the individual cords on individual yarn bobbins, (2) wrapping each cord around a piece of cardboard and securing the cord with a rubber band (note the indentation on either end of the cardboard to prevent slippage), and (3) creating a butterfly. If the cord is to be folded in half, begin wrapping the cord from each end toward the folded end of the cord.

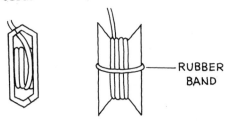

RUBBER
BAND

RUBBER
BAND

BASIC KNOTS

Overhand Knot

1   Knot each end of the Holding Cord with an Overhand Knot. To make an Overhand Knot, cross the cord over itself. Put the tail of the cord under and through the loop that is formed.

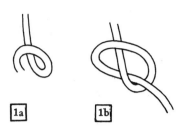

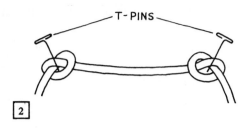

2 Using T-pins, pin each knotted end to your board or pillow.

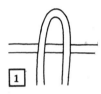

Lark's Head Knot

1 Fold the cord in half that is to become the Lark's Head. Place the folded end of the cord on top of the Holding Cord.

2 Bend the folded loop back over the Holding Cord.

3 Put the two tails of the looped cord through the looped part.

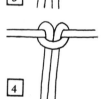

4 Pull the two tails tightly to form the Lark's Head.

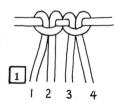

Square Knot

1 Start out with four cords. The four cords may be the ends of two Lark's Heads.

2   Lay cord 1 on top of cords 2 and 3 and under cord 4.

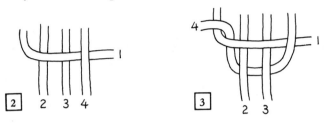

3   Put cord 4 underneath cords 3 and 2, behind, up through, and on top of cord 1.

4   Pull both cord 1 and cord 4 to tighten the cords, while holding tightly to the two other cords. You now have half a Square Knot.

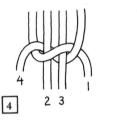 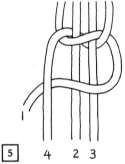

5   Take cord 1 and place it on top of cords 3 and 2 and under cord 4.

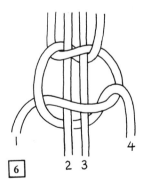

6   Put cord 4 under cords 2 and 3 and behind, up through, and on top of cord 1.

90 MACRAMÉ

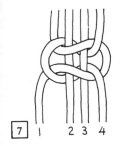

7 Pull cords 1 and 4 to tighten the knot. You will notice in the finished knot that the cord that went on top of the two center cords (2 and 3) for the first half of the knot is also on top of the two center cords in the second half of the knot.

Double Half Hitch

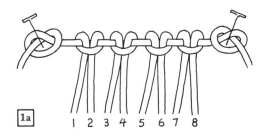

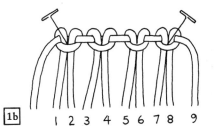

1 Fold one of your cords in half to make a Holding Cord. Put two Overhand Knots in the center of this Holding Cord about 5 inches apart from each other. Pin this cord to a board or pillow and, using the Lark's Head Knot, attach the desired number of cords to it. Leave a space between each Lark's Head because in working the Double Half Hitch, the width of the piece is made wider by the Double Half Hitch. Remove the two Overhand Knots in the Holding Cord and put the T-pins through the center of each of the outer Lark's Head Knots as shown in the drawing on the right.

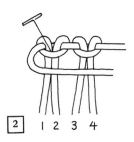

2 Place the left end of the Holding Cord horizontally on top of the cords that are to be used for making the Double Half Hitch. Hold the end of the Holding Cord in one hand while you make the Double Half Hitch with the other hand.

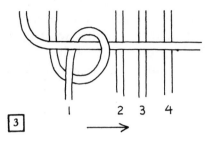

3   Bring the lower end of cord 1 up and over the Holding Cord, then down to the left behind the Holding Cord.

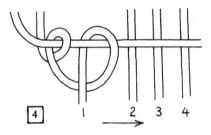

4   For the second half of the knot bring cord 1 up and over the Holding Cord, then down to the left behind the Holding Cord and on top of the loop formed.

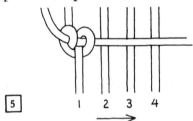

5   Pull the cord tightly to create the two loops on the Holding Cord. The Holding Cord must be held tightly when this is done, or the Holding Cord will become looped. Then go on to cord 2.

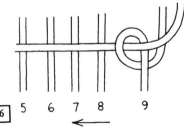

6   When working from left to right, place cord 9 up and over the Holding Cord, then down to the right behind the Holding Cord.

92 MACRAMÉ

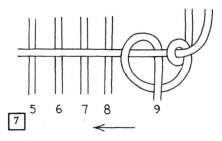

5 6 7 8   9

[7]   ←

7   For the second half of the knot place cord 9 up and over the Holding Cord, then down to the right behind the Holding Cord and on top of the loop formed.

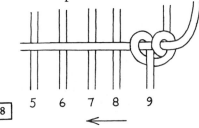

5   6   7 8   9

[8]   ←

8   Pull the cord tightly to create the two loops on the Holding Cord. Then go on to the next cord, cord 8. NOTE: Diagonal Double Half Hitches are made by putting the Holding Cord at the angle desired.

Cavandoli Stitch

The Cavandoli Stitch utilizes both the Horizontal Double Half Hitch explained above and the Vertical Double Half Hitch. Designs or patterns are created by using a Holding Cord of one color and the other cords of another color. Designs are planned on graph paper, with each square representing a Double Half Hitch Knot. A series of Lark's Head Knots are usually placed on the Holding Cord to start this work.

1   Design a pattern on graph paper. Use an even number of squares, because each Lark's Head Knot has two cords. In this design, 64 squares are used across the design horizontally. This

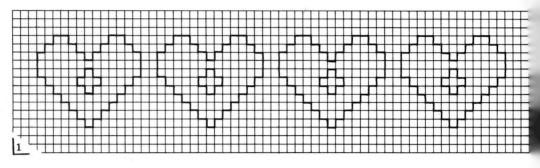

means that 32 Lark's Head Knots must be put on the Holding Cord. If Square Knots were to follow below this design, there would be 16 Square Knots, with each knot consisting of four cords.

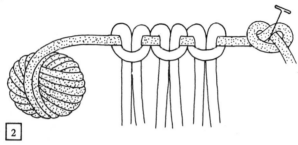

2   Attach the cords to the Holding Cord using the Lark's Head Knot. Each Lark's Head Knot counts for two squares on the graph paper because it contains two cords. The Holding Cord should be very long and rolled into a ball.

3   Follow the steps for a Double Half Hitch (Steps 2 to 5) when working from left to right. This will create a Horizontal Double Half Hitch.

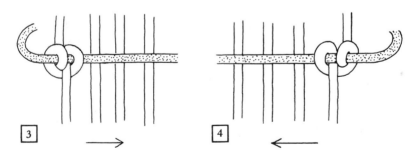

4   After you finish row 1, work from right to left to return. Follow steps 6 to 8 for the Double Half Hitch.

94 MACRAMÉ

5   To make a knot the color of the Holding Cord when working from left to right, put the Holding Cord behind the Double Half Hitch Cord.

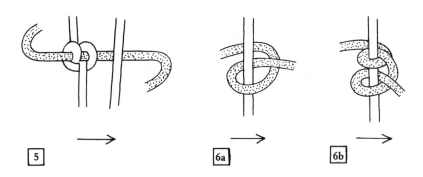

6   Loop the Holding Cord from right to left on top of the Double Half Hitch Cord and behind it to the right and on top of itself. Repeat this step again for the second half of the Vertical Double Half Hitch.

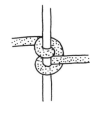

7   Pull the Holding Cord tightly to create the two loops. Continue in this fashion when moving from left to right.

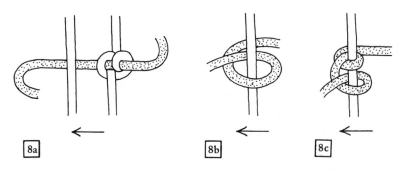

8   When moving from right to left, place the Holding Cord underneath the Double Half Hitch Cord. Loop the Holding Cord from left to right on top of the Double Half Hitch Cord and behind it to the right and on top of itself. Repeat this step again for the second half of the Vertical Double Half Hitch.

9 Pull the Holding Cord tightly to create the two loops. Continue in this fashion when moving from right to left.

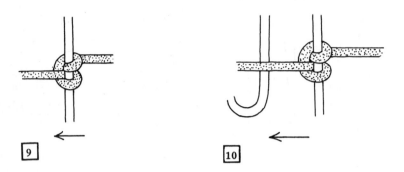

10 If the next knot is to be the color of the Double Half Hitch cord, place the Holding Cord *on top of* the Double Half Hitch Cord and repeat step 4 above (See steps 6 to 8 for the Double Half Hitch).

PLANNING DESIGNS

In creating a pattern for macramé, two things must first be considered: (1) the types of knots that are to be used, and (2) the final size of the piece. The types of knots that are used will determine how many cords you will need horizontally. The final size of the piece will determine how long these cords need to be. There are two variables that will also influence your work: (1) how tightly you knot, and (2) the type of cord you use. If you knot tightly, you will use less cord and your piece will be smaller than anticipated. If you use a small type of cord, such as crochet cotton, your piece will be smaller than if you were to use a cotton rug yarn.

If you plan to use Square Knots, you will need four cords for each Square Knot. If you use a Holding Cord and attach Lark's Head Knots on it, you will obtain two cords for each Lark's Head Knot and also two cords from each end of your Holding Cord, or one end from your Holding Cord, if you desire. In the Cavandoli Stitch it is possible that the Holding Cord would not be counted as a cord. It can be ended once that part of the design has been completed.

Once you have determined how many cords you will need, the next step is to determine the length of your finished piece. Work a small sample area of some cords to determine how many rows you will need for a given length for the type of cord you are using. This will help you plan your pattern better. Follow the method for determining the amount of cord needed that was given in the General Preparation section of this chapter.

You may develop your own symbols to indicate the type of knot you plan to make, or you may use the symbols suggested here. When writing down directions to yourself, use the first letters of the knot indicated.

⊎	⊕	LH	LARK'S HEAD
✕	☐	SK	SQUARE KNOT
⊞	⊕	HDHH	HORIZONTAL DOUBLE HALF HITCH
⊟	⊖	VDHH	VERTICAL DOUBLE HALF HITCH

Each cord should be indicated by a line leading to the knot you plan to do. Often designs are not written down, but are developed freely as the work progresses. This method leads to a much more free and creative macramé piece.

BELT

If the belt is to be 36 inches long when completed, multiply 36 by 4 and then multiply by 2 because each cord is folded in half for the Lark's Head. That would be 288 inches, or 24 feet, or 8 yards for *each cord.* You will need 8 yards multiplied by 8 cords or 64 yards for the belt. If you knot your cords close together, multiply 36 by 5 and then multiply by 2. That would make each cord 360 inches or 30 feet or 10 yards for *each cord.* You will need 10 yards multiplied by 8 cords or 80 yards to make the belt if your knots are close together.

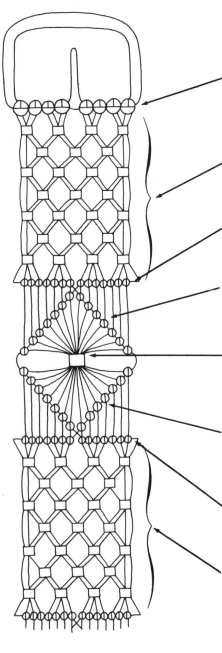

1   Attach 8 cords to a buckle using LH knot.

2   Make 7 rows of alternating SK.

3   Bring each outer cord to the center. Place 7 HDHH horizontally on each outer cord.

4   Cross the two Holding Cords and place 7 HDHH diagonally on each Holding Cord.

5   Use the two end cords just inside the two Holding Cords to make a SK, gathering the other 10 cords to the center of the SK. (This is called the Gathering Knot.)

6   Bring the Holding Cords on either end to the center to form the bottom half of the diamond and place 7 HDHH diagonally on each Holding Cord.

7   Cross the two Holding Cords and put 7 HDHH horizontally on each Holding Cord.

8   Repeat 7 rows of alternating SK.

9   Repeat steps 3 to 8 until belt is the desired length.

10   When you cut your cords, weave the loose ends back into the piece (A crochet hook can be used to pull the cords back through the knots on the backside.) and secure them with white glue.

As a general rule, if you make an error in macramé, be consistent and continue the error, or unknot your piece and reknot it correctly. However, by following the error, you can often create a new knot. Experiment with knots. Try, for example, doing a row of Horizontal Double Half Hitches across eight cords and then bring the Holding Cord across the back of these cords and pull it tightly so that the cords form a cylinder and then put the Holding Cord on top of the first cord and make a Double Half Hitch. This will create a spiralling Horizontal Double Half Hitch as you work horizontally around this group of cords. When you make a series of Square Knots one directly below the other, leave large loops made with the two outer cords between the Square Knots. In another experiment take the center two cords of a series of Square Knots one underneath the other and pull them through the center of the first Square Knot. This creates a raised three-dimensional area. Using styrofoam blocks or styrofoam wig heads, work your macramé cords three-dimensionally around the forms to create sculptures in macramé. Try using two cords where one cord is called for. With the three basic knots you have learned in this chapter you can develop many more simply by experimenting with the cords you are using.

eight

WEAVING

The chapter opening shows a woven piece created by Karen Enos on a box loom.

Weaving is a very ancient craft that probably developed when people first tried plaiting reeds and plant fibers together. In different parts of the world there developed a variety of ways of making looms for holding fibers while passing other fibers over and under them. The fabrics that developed ranged from the lightweight transparent fabrics of Egypt and Greece to the heavy brocades of the Orient.

Fabric woven on a loom consists primarily of two types of threads. The warp threads are those threads that run from top to bottom, or vertically, and they are usually the strongest threads of the piece or are of the same strength as the strongest weft threads that are used. The weft, woof, or filling threads are those threads that run across the loom from left to right, or horizontally. In weaving it is necessary to raise some of the warp threads while leaving others unraised. This creates a *shed* or opening between the warp threads. In order to raise some of the warp threads, a *harness* is used. A harness is an open frame containing many *heddles*. Heddles may be wires that have a hole

A woven hanging by Jean Williams, of raffia warp and weft, created on the backstrap loom with plaiting used to hold the four sections together.

This wall hanging by Marilyn Ambrosio, woven on a back-strap loom, shows the use of the tapestry technique to create zigzag areas in the bottom half of the wall hanging.

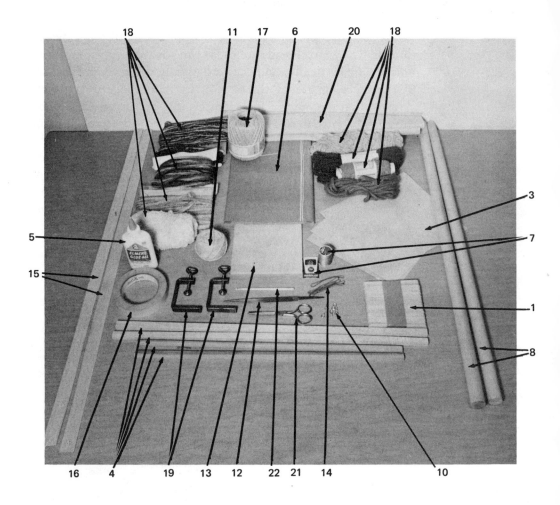

Supplies for Backstrap Loom	Sources of Supplies*
1. 20-30 popsicle sticks or coffee stirrers 2. Drill press and drill (not shown) 3. Sandpaper 4. 4 strips of wood $\frac{1}{2}$-inch wide by $\frac{1}{8}$-$\frac{1}{4}$-inch thick by 12-14 inches long 5. White glue 6. 2 strips of denim 7 inches by 27 inches 7. Needle and thread 8. Two 1-inch dowel sticks, approximately 24 inches long 9. Coping saw (not shown) 10. 6 screw eyes 11. Twine 12. Triangular file 13. 6 inches by 6 inches by $\frac{1}{4}$-inch thick piece of wood for shuttles 14. Rubberbands 15. 2 narrow strips of wood 1 inch wide by 14 inches long ∕or 2 rulers 16. Masking tape	Commercial looms can be obtained from the following sources listed in Appendix B: BG, CH, JLH, LMC, MAA, NLC, SAC, and TYD. Yarns can be obtained from the following sources listed in Appendix B: BI, CH, CY, JLH, LMC, SAC, and TYD

NOTE: 1-16 can be omitted if a commercial loom and shuttles are published.

17. Crochet cotton
18. Yarns
19. C-clamps
20. 2 strips of fabric 8 inches wide by 14 inches long
21. Scissors
22. Crochet hook

*Letters refer to mail order outlets listed in *Appendix B: Addresses of Suppliers.*

in the center through which a warp thread passes. There are usually two or more harnesses on a loom in order to create at least two sheds. A shuttle carries the weft thread across the loom, and a reed or beater placed in front of the harness straightens the weft threads. If a plain weave is desired, every other warp thread is passed through a heddle in the first harness; the warp threads not passed through heddles in the first harness are passed through the heddles in the second harness. The plain weave is used in making tapestries. Patterns in weaving are created by the number of warp threads that consecutively pass through the heddles of each of the harnesses used. Patterns for the heddles and harnesses can be drafted on graph paper.

The greatest fun and excitement of weaving occurs in the selection and weaving of the variety of materials that are available. Materials range from narrow metallic threads to fluffy, thick wools and natural materials such as leaves, reeds, and seed pods. Variation in the types of materials used and also in the methods of weaving creates visual interest. Yarns can be looped and tufted besides being woven in different patterns.

There are many projects that you can make on a loom. They vary from simple belts to complex tapestries. You can make necklaces, purses, shoulder strap bags, pillows, upholstery, scarves, stoles, placemats, table runners, table cloths, rugs, ponchos, and bedspreads. Although weaving is primarily a two-dimensional craft, it is possible, even on a backstrap loom, to create three-dimensional weavings.

This woven hanging by Jean Williams, of wool warp and weft, was created on the backstrap loom. It was woven from the center of the warp towards the ends. Plaiting was used in the center to help form the shape of the weaving.

LOOMS

There are many types of looms that can be used for weaving. The idea is to create some kind of apparatus that will hold a given number of threads stable while other threads are interlocked with them. Below are some suggestions for simple, easy to make, and easy to use looms.

1   A very simple loom consists of a piece of corrugated
cardboard with a single row of pins spaced about ¼-inch apart
from each other across the top edge. The warp threads are
wound around the pin and then around the cardboard and then
back around the same pin from the opposite side. The thread is
then carried around the cardboard and wound around the next
pin, around the cardboard and back around the same pin from
the opposite side. This is continued until all the pins have
thread wound around them from both sides. The weaving is
begun with the weft thread across the bottom edge of the loom,
which can become the bottom of a purse. The weft is woven
around the loom in a circular manner. It is easier to weave the
weft threads over and under the warp threads near the top edge
of the loom if a needle rather than a bobbin is used. From the
simple loom, you can make a woven clutch bag or the bag part
of a shoulder strap bag.

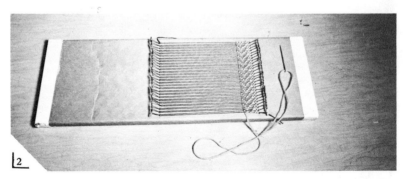

2   You can construct another very simple loom by using pins
on a yardage bolt. Place the pins about ¼-inch apart from each
other at opposite ends of the length of the yardage bolt and the

length and width that you desire. Wrap heavy twine from one
end to the other around each pin. You can weave a simple place
mat on such a loom.

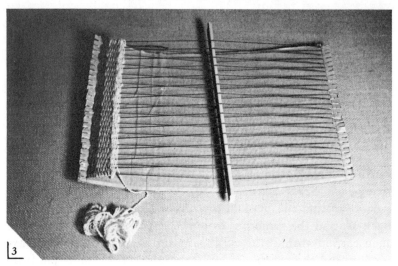

3   You can clip the ends of a piece of cardboard and wrap
cord from one end to the other to make a bowed cardboard
loom.

4   You can construct a box loom from four slats of wood
with nails positioned ¼-inch apart from each other on both
ends, around which you can wind the warp threads.

All of these looms are referred to as *rigid looms* or looms for finger weaving. Looms that have a way of raising and lowering the warp threads to create a shed are called *flexible looms*. The backstrap loom, which will be shown in this chapter, is a flexible loom and can be easily constructed. Another flexible loom is the Inkle loom. Both of these looms have heddles that permit the warp threads to be raised and lowered to create sheds for easy weaving.

BACKSTRAP LOOM WEAVING

Making the Harness

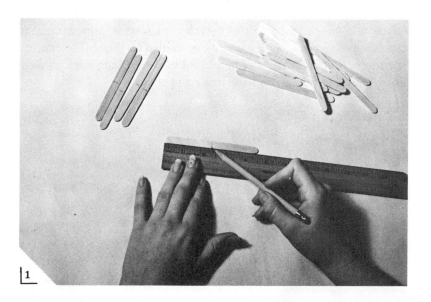

1   Gather twenty to thirty popsicle sticks. Mark the center of each stick. In the center of each stick drill a hole the size of the yarn you plan to use. File and sand this hole and sand the side edges of each stick. This is necessary so that your yarn will not become frayed and weakened by catching on the rough wood.

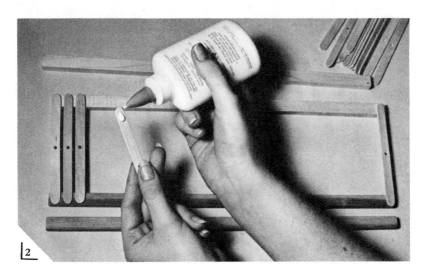

2   Cut four strips of wood approximately ½-inch wide by ⅛-
or ¼-inch thick by 12 to 14 inches long. The length can vary
depending on how wide you want your piece to be. Lay two of
the strips of wood parallel to each other and close enough
together so that the top and bottom of the popsicle sticks rest
on top of the two strips. Glue all the sticks to the two wood
strips, allowing a space between each stick that is approximately
the same size as the holes you have drilled in them. The reason
for this is that the yarn will be placed between each stick as well
as through the holes you have drilled in them.

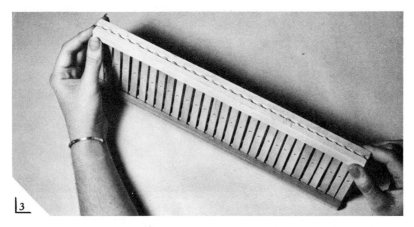

3   Glue the other two strips on top of the popsicle sticks so
that they are sandwiched between the two wooden strips on the
top and on the bottom. This makes the harness that will raise
and lower the warp threads.

Making the Backstrap

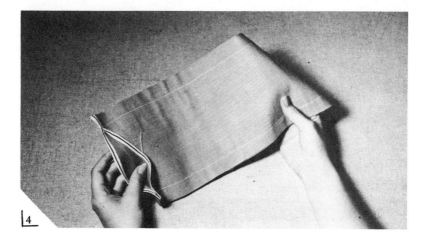

4   Cut two strips of denim or other heavy weight fabric 7 inches by 27 inches. Put the right sides of the fabric together and sew along the long sides about 1 inch in from the edges.

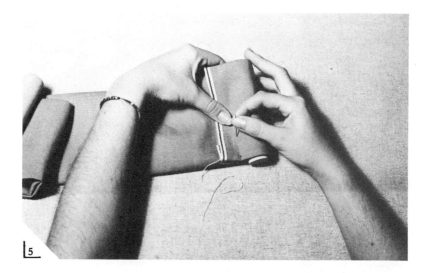

5   Turn the fabric right side out. Cut two 1-inch dowel sticks or strips of wood the length of the short sides of your fabric. Fold the fabric of the short side over one dowel stick and pin or baste along the line that you will sew to enclose the dowel stick. Sew the ends down.

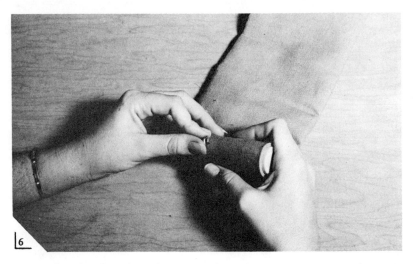

6   Slip the dowel stick into each end. Put a screw eye through the fabric in the center of each dowel stick.

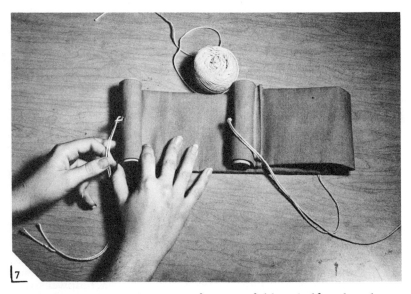

7   Cut two 24-inch strips of twine; fold in half and make a Lark's Head (see Macramé chapter) through the screw eye. This string will be tied later to the wooden dowel holding the warp threads.

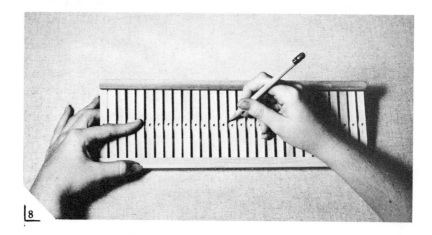

8   Cut two 1-inch dowel sticks the length of your harness. Place the harness over each dowel stick and mark the location of each hole and slot beginning and ending with the holes in the first and last popsicle sticks.

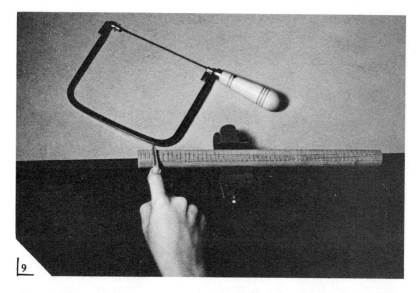

9   With a coping saw, saw a 1-inch long groove for each hole and slot you marked on the dowel stick, and then, using a triangular file, widen each groove made by the coping saw.

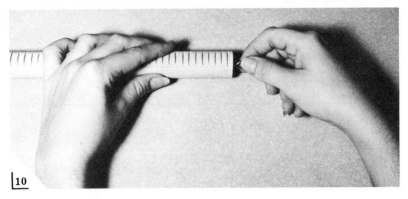

10 Put a screw eye at the end of each dowel stick. Your sticks are now ready for you to put the yarn or twine (warp threads) on them.

Preparing the Warp

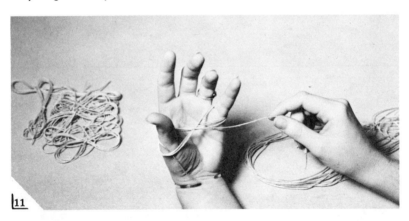

11 Decide on the length of your warp threads. Allow 12 inches extra on each end for a total of 24 extra inches. Place C-clamps a yard apart and wind each warp thread around the C-clamps once for each yard or use a warping board. Cut the warp thread when the desired length has been reached. Wrap each thread around your hand in a butterfly (see Macramé chapter). Set each warp thread aside until it is time to warp the loom.

Attaching the Warp

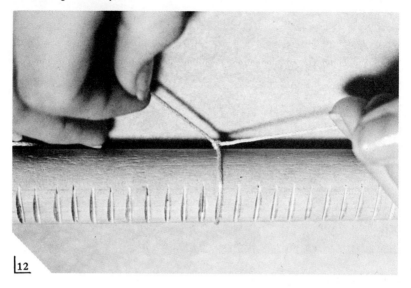

12

12   Tie one end of each warp thread onto one of the grooved dowel sticks. The groove will prevent the warp from slipping from side to side. Use a Double Half Hitch done with the short end of the thread. The Double Half Hitch is illustrated above (refer to the Macramé chapter for directions).

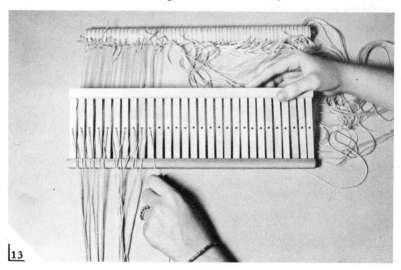

13

13   After all the warp threads have been tied onto one dowel stick, put each warp thread through either a hole or a slot in the harness you have made. Start with the first hole you drilled in the popsicle stick.

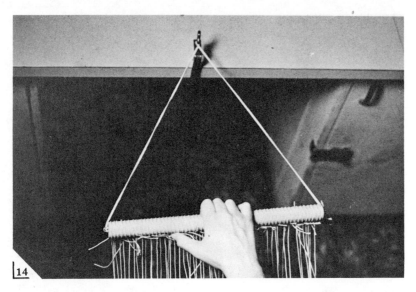

14 Tie a piece of twine through the screw eyes of the dowel stick that has the warp on it. Loop this twine over a C-clamp placed at seated eye level.

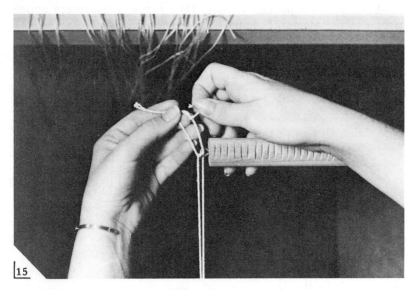

15 When all the warp threads have been put through the harness, put the backstrap around the back of your waist and tie the strings from each end of the backstrap onto the screw eye at each end of the dowel stick that does not have the warp on it.

16 Sitting down, tie the first warp thread on the left to the dowel stick that has been attached to the backstrap. Use the Double Half Hitch that you used in step 12. Tie the last warp thread on your right to the dowel stick that has been attached to the backstrap. Try to have the first and last warp threads the same length from the top dowel stick to the bottom dowel stick nearest to you and have all the warp threads under the same tension. You may need another person to hold the harness for you while tying the warp threads to prevent the weight of the harness from pulling down on the warp threads. Continue tying on the warp threads one at a time, working first on the left side and then on the right side. Try to keep the tension of all the warp threads the same. If the threads are of different tensions, when the weaving is removed from the loom the warp threads will pull the weft threads up in a wavy pattern instead of the even horizontal line that is desired. It is also a good idea to try to keep all the knots on the dowel stick in the same position so that if they slip and release the tension of a warp thread, this will be noticed and can be corrected.

Preparing the Shuttle

17 Cut a strip of wood for each different color or type of yarn you will be weaving. Cut a ¼-inch thick strip of wood approximately 2 inches wide by 6 inches long. Cut and sand a

17

U-shaped notch in each end. Wind the desired yarn securely around the U-shaped ends. A rubber band may be used to hold the yarn in the center of the shuttle.

Beginning the Weaving

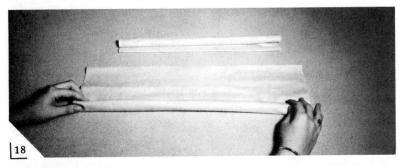

18

18 Cut two strips of fabric 8 inches wide by the length of your dowel sticks. Roll each strip of fabric into a cylinder that is the length of your dowel sticks.

19 Lift your harness up. This separates your warp threads and creates the first shed. Place one of your fabric forms through this shed and about 6 inches up from the dowel stick that is nearest to you. The fabric should be parallel to the dowel sticks.

19

Straighten the fabric by allowing the harness to resume its natural position in the center of the warp and pull it against the fabric cylinder, which has been flattened by the warp threads.

20

20 Move your harness back to the center of the loom and push it down. This creates the second shed. Place your second fabric cylinder above the first one and through the second shed you have made. Pull the harness toward the fabric form and beat it against the fabric as before.

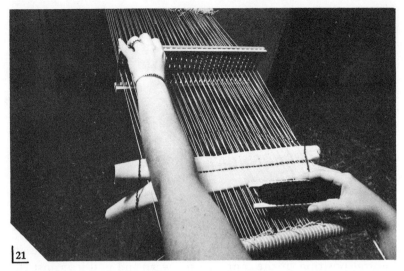

21   Unwind enough yarn from your shuttle to go across all the warp threads and have 6 inches left as a tail. Lift up your harness to create the first shed. Place the shuttle through the first shed and pull the yarn through this shed, creating a narrow arch with your weft yarn or filling. Let 6 inches of yarn hang down on the opposite end. This may be knotted with the Overhand Knot on the warp thread that is near this end, or it may be pulled up parallel to the warp thread and woven into the piece as you progress. Pull the harness toward you to straighten out the warp thread you have just put in. The harness should be pulled forward quickly and parallel to the dowel sticks and then returned to the center of the loom.

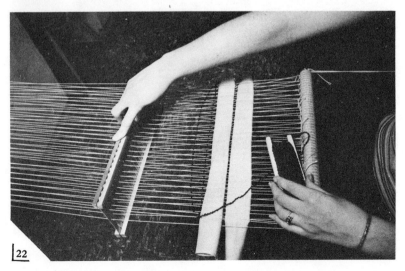

22 Push the harness down to create the second shed. Pass your shuttle through the shed, forming a small arch with the filling. Pull the harness toward you quickly to straighten the warp thread. Continue this process until you have filled in the area desired.

Shortening the Warp

23 When it becomes difficult to reach to the area you are weaving, roll up the warp to bring the weaving area closer to you. First, remove the fabric forms, then cut two narrow strips of wood approximately 1½ to 2 inches wide by the length of your dowel sticks, or you could use rulers that are the length of the width of your weaving. Place one of the sticks of wood underneath the dowel stick nearest to you.

24 Roll the woven area over and under this wooden stick and the dowel stick. Place the second wooden stick on top of the other wooden stick, and, using a rubber band, secure the ends of both the wooden sticks and the dowel stick. You will need to

remove the twine from the two ends of the dowel stick temporarily in order to do this. Replace the twine on the two ends of the dowel stick and attach the twine to the screw eyes on the backstrap. You are now ready to continue weaving.

Piecing the Weft

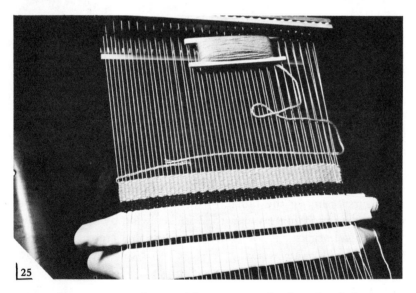

25 When you need to add a new weft thread of the same color, use the same shed that you just finished with and insert the new weft thread so that it overlaps about six or eight warp threads that have the end of the last weft thread on them. After you finish that row, change the shed and continue weaving.

Changing the Color of the Weft

26 For a tapestry effect or to change the color of the weft when the two different colors meet in the same shed, loop one color through the other and turn the yarn back on itself in the new shed. In a second method, you can loop the yarn back on itself in the new shed and sew up the gap or relay between the two colors using a similarly colored thread after the weaving has been completed.

27 If you are weaving short bands of the same color, carry the yarn up to the next section by running it parallel to the end warp thread. When changing the weft color for a wide section,

conceal the tail either in the same shed as the first row of the new color, or pull the tail up and parallel to the end warp thread of the new color section.

Completing the Weaving

28   When you have finished weaving, remove the rulers or sticks on which the weaving has been rolled and unroll the weaving. Untie the warp threads, working from the center to the edges.

29   Double knot two warp ends across the top and bottom of the woven piece. Using a crochet hook, you may pull the warp ends up through the weft threads and parallel to the warp threads, or you may knot the ends to form a decorative fringe on the two ends of the woven piece. This piece has Square Knots across the top and bottom and is hung from a coat hanger that has had the metal hook removed from it.

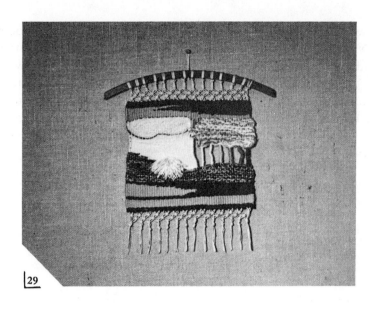

29

FURTHER SUGGESTIONS

Warp threads can be twisted and the yarn woven through the twisted sections. Several warp threads can be pulled together and wrapped with yarn as was done in the project illustrated here. Try weaving three different strands of yarn at the same time, treating them as one weft thread. Create patterns by going over two threads instead of one and in the next row repeat the same thing but start out by going over one and then under two and over one. After about four rows of progressing one warp thread ahead, reverse what you have been doing. A zigzag or chevron pattern can be created in this fashion. Try sewing contrasting threads under, over, and around a woven weft thread and the warp threads. Tufts of yarn can be made by cutting a strip of yarn about 4 inches long and laying it horizontally over two warp threads. Then pull the two ends through the loom, around the two warp threads, and up between the two warp threads in the center. Continue across the loom in this fashion. In the second row use one warp thread of each of two sets of warp threads that have tufts of yarn on them and proceed across the second row, creating alternating tufts. When you have finished the tufted area, trim with a scissors to the desired height. Weft threads do not always have to be woven in a straight line; they can be arched and filled in.

The weaving does not have to progress straight across the loom, covering all the warp threads; the weft threads can be returned and woven back and forth in one area, leaving exposed warp threads in another. As you experiment with the weft thread, looping it around a pencil while you progress across the loom, or looping it around a warp thread, many other ideas will come to you. Each will provide you with many fascinating hours of weaving.

nine

ACRYLIC CASTING

The cast acrylic pin by the author, shown on the preceding page, has been enhanced by the addition of Inca burial beads suspended from it.

You can obtain acrylic resin and many of the other supplies you will need for this craft from dental supply houses. Dental repair acrylic consists of two parts: a powdered form (a polymer) and a liquid form (a monomer). The polymer is the chemically cross-linked (cured part), and the monomer is not cross-linked (the uncured part) and acts as an agent (a catalyst) to bind the polymer and monomer together. The powdered form of the dental repair acrylic is available in a clear form or in pink tones. Powdered tooth shade acrylic can be used to create tones varying from white to beige. You can obtain powdered acrylic dyes from acrylic dye suppliers. When requesting dye samples, be sure to mention the type of acrylic you are using because different types of resin monomer will affect the dyes differently; for example, they may burn out a blue color so that no trace of blue is seen. These powdered dyes are mixed with a little of the liquid acrylic (monomer) before the liquid acrylic is mixed with the powdered acrylic. It is also possible to mix dry materials in the clear powdered acrylic before adding the liquid acrylic; gold leaf, metallic powders, and dried spices (except those that will dissolve) may be used. Many liquid dyes, such as polyester resin dyes, will inhibit the curing of the acrylic resin, so powdered dyes are usually used.

This pendent by Richard Takashima shows the use of orégano inside the acrylic casting to give it color and texture.

This belt buckle, created and modeled by Wendy Stanton, can be a versatile piece.

This bicycle pin by Jaime Stone shows the technique of painting on the acrylic casting between layers of acrylic.

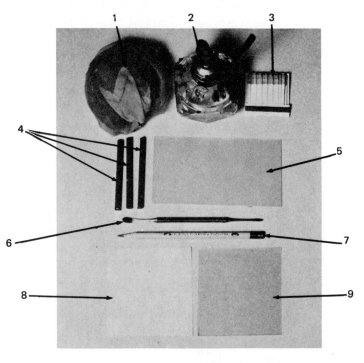

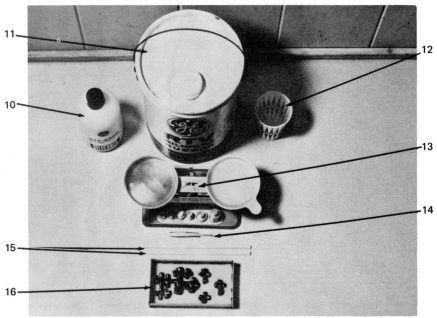

Supplies for Wax Model	Sources of Supplies*
1. Nylon stocking	
2. Alcohol lamp	2. ATS, BAC, BG, CCI, CRH, EH, GG, JLH, MAC, SAC, SI, TAC, Dental supply houses
3. Matches	
4. Inlay casting wax	4. ATS, CCI, CRH, GG, MAC, SAC, Dental supply houses
5. Base plate wax	5. ATS, CCI, CRH, GG, MAC, Dental supply houses
6. Dental spatula	6. CCI, CRH, EH, GG, MAC, SAC, Dental supply houses
7. Pencil	
8. Paper	
9. Sheet wax (22 or 24 gauge)	9. ATS, CCI, CRH, GG, MAC, SAC, Dental supply houses

*Letters refer to mail order outlets listed in *Appendix B: Addresses of Suppliers.*

Supplies for Silicone Mold	Sources of Supplies*
10. Silicone Rubber (B part)	10. CRH, ESC
11. Silicone Rubber (A part)	11. CRH, ESC
12. Paper cup	
13. Gram scale	13. CCI, CRH, MAC, Ceramic suppliers, Chemical supply houses
14. Tweezers for picking up weights	
15. Chop sticks	
16. Wax model	

*Letters refer to mail order outlets listed in *Appendix B: Addresses of Suppliers.*

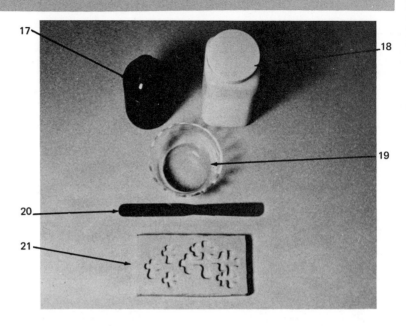

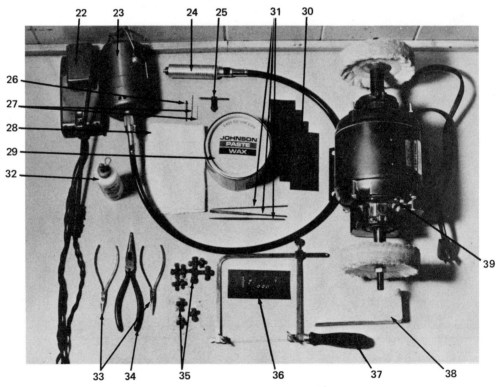

Supplies for Acrylic Casting	Sources of Supplies*
17. Dental repair acrylic (liquid form)	17. Dental supply houses
18. Dental repair acrylic (powdered form)	18. Dental supply houses
19. Glass dish	
20. Enameling spatula	20. AAC, ATS, CRH, JLH, TAC, TCT, WCS
21. Silicone rubber mold	

Refining Acrylic Casting	Sources of Supplies *
22. Flexible shaft (foot pedal)	22.-25. ATS, BG, CCI, CRH, GG, MAC, SAC, SI, Dental supply houses
23. Flexible shaft (motor)	
24. Flexible shaft (head)	
25. Key for adjusting head of flexible shaft	
26. Metal burr (high speed)	26. ATS, CCI, CRH, GG, MAC, SAC, SI
27. High speed drills	27. ATS, BG, CCI, CRH, GG, MAC, SI, Hardware stores
28. Flannel	
29. Paste wax	
30. Wet/Dry sandpaper	
31. Needle files	31. ATS, BAC, BG, CCI, CRH, GG, JLH, MAC, SAC, SI, TAC, WCS
32. Casein base glue	
33. Jeweler's pliers	33. ATS, BAC, BG, CCI, CRH, GG, JLH, MAC, SI, TAC, WCS
34. Wire cutting pliers	34. AH, BAC, CCI, CRH, MAC, TAC, WCS, Hardware stores
35. Acrylic casting	
36. Findings	36. ATS, GG, SI
37. Jeweler's saw and saw blade	37. AH, ATS, BAC, BG, CCI, CRH, JLH, MAC, SAC, SI, TAC, TCT, WCS
38. Aluminum oxide buffing compound or Tripoli	38. ATS, BAC, CCI, CRH, GG, SAC, SI, TAC
39. Buffer	39. BAC, BG, CCI, CRH, GG, MAC, SAC, Hardware stores

*Letters refer to mail order outlets listed in *Appendix B: Addresses of Suppliers.*

Although the method described in the following pages will work if you use polyester resin, acrylic resin was chosen for the following reasons:

1. Acrylic resin, when cured, has a better impact strength than polyester resin. If you drop your acrylic casting, it will be less likely to break than if it were a polyester casting.
2. Polyester resin will permeate the silicone mold and eventually will cause the mold to become rigid, but acrylic resin does not do this.
3. Acrylic resin cures with less problems than polyester resin. Polyester castings tend to develop tacky surfaces where they are exposed to air during the curing process, and the castings may crack if too much catalyst is used. These problems do not occur with acrylic castings.

The four major steps involved in making an acrylic casting are: (1) creating the wax model; (2) making the silicone mold; (3) casting the acrylic resin; and (4) refining the casting.

PRECAUTIONS

The liquid part of the acrylic casting material is highly flammable and should be handled very carefully: keep the liquid resin away from open flames and burning cigarettes. Breathing the fumes of acrylic resin during the casting process may cause kidney problems; make sure that your work area is well-ventilated.

PROCEDURE

Creating the Design and Preparing the Wax Model

1   Draw your design on a sheet of paper. Create a design that has rounded rather than angular corners. REASON: Sometimes, in the casting process, the acrylic will not flow into an angular corner. After you have created your design, lay a sheet of sheet

wax over your design and, using a dental spatula, cut out your design. If there are to be openings in the final piece, make these depressions rather than openings cut all the way through. REASON: As the acrylic cures, it shrinks and would crack apart around the opening where the silicone mold material is.

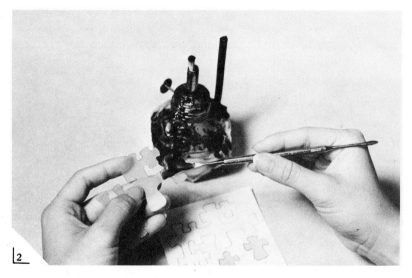

2   Attach a stick of inlay casting wax to an alcohol lamp. Heat the dental spatula and melt the inlay casting wax onto the dental spatula. Reheat the dental spatula and flow the inlay casting wax onto the sheet wax model. Build up the model to a thickness of approximately $^3/_8$ inch. Wax the back side as you wax the front side. REASON: The model will curl and become distorted if you work on only one side at a time.

3   Attach your wax model to a nonporous surface (base plate wax, glass, or plastic) by allowing the inlay casting wax from the dental spatula to flow between the model and the nonporous surface. The nonporous surface will become the bottom of a container for your wax model and for the silicone rubber mold you will cast (steps 5 to 11). Use an old nylon stocking to polish the surface of your wax model. If some areas need to be smoothed more, use a heavier rubbing technique to create friction to melt the surface, and then polish the surface by buffing lightly with the nylon stocking.

4   Cut the walls for the model's container from the base plate wax and attach them to the nonporous surface by using the dental spatula to apply the inlay casting wax to join the walls to the base of the container. Wax both the inner and outer edges where the wax walls are joined to the base.

5

5   The silicone mold you will make consists of a two-part room temperature vulcanizing (RTV) silicone material. The material cures at room temperature and does not need to be heated. One part (B) of this material is a catalyst that activates the other part (A) and causes it to cure or solidify. After the silicone has been mixed, it should be placed in a vacuum to remove any air bubbles in the material. Step 9 shows an alternative way to do this if the equipment to create a vacuum is not available to remove the air bubbles. In preparation for making the silicone mold, place a container on the gram scale and balance its weight.

6

6   Place weights on the gram scale for measuring the A part of the silicone rubber. Mix the silicone rubber (RTV-630 by

General Electric is being used here) using ten parts of A to one part of B. A is pictured in photo 6.

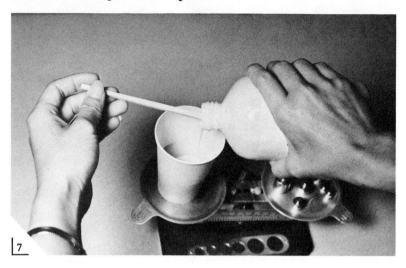

7   Add weights to create the ratio necessary for the one part of B. Then add one part of B to the ten parts of A in the cup.

8   Mix the two parts of the silicone rubber thoroughly and *slowly* to avoid stirring in air bubbles. Since the two parts are different colors (the RTV-630 A is blue, and the RTV-630 B is white), it is easy to tell when they are mixed. After the two parts are mixed, pour the silicone rubber over the prepared wax model in its box container.

9   Drop the container gently up and down on a flat surface to make the air bubbles in the mixture rise to the surface and pop open.

Cleaning the Silicone Mold

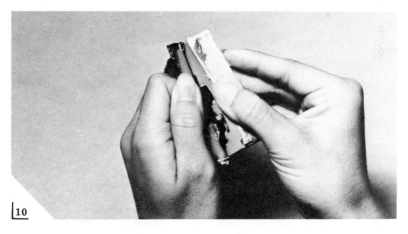

10   After allowing the silicone rubber mixture to set for 24 hours at room temperature, remove the sides of the wax container. Remove the wax model from the silicone mold.

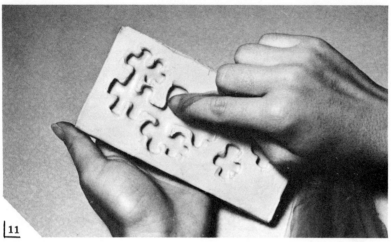

11

11 Clean the silicone mold thoroughly with an old nylon stocking to remove the small pieces of wax. REASON: The pieces of wax will show in the acrylic casting if they are not removed.

Casting the Acrylic Resin

12 Pour dental repair acrylic or tooth shade cold cure acrylic (powdered form) into a glass container in preparation for the casting.

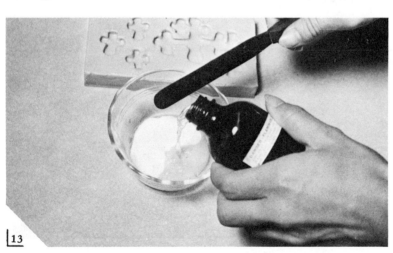

12

13

13 Mix the dental repair acrylic or cold cure tooth acrylic (liquid form) with the acrylic powder. The liquid acrylic is highly flammable; avoid having open flames or lighted cigarettes around while the casting is being done. The fumes are toxic, so casting should be done in a well-ventilated area.

14 Pour the acrylic mixture into the silicone mold and allow it to harden. This process takes about 20 minutes, depending on the amount of liquid in the mixture. If a large amount of liquid has been used, it will take longer to set.

Refining the Casting

15 After the mixture has hardened, remove the cast acrylic piece from the silicone mold.

16 Using a jeweler's saw, remove the flash on the cast acrylic piece. Flash is the extra acrylic that is around the edges of the casting. If you have been careful in pouring your acrylic, there will be no flash material.

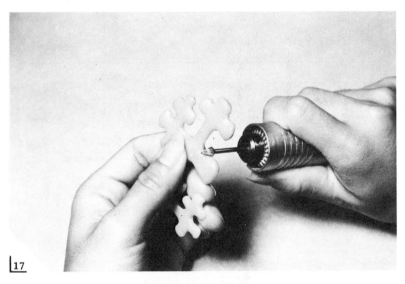

17 Shape the edges of the casting with a flexible shaft that has a high speed metal burr in it. Wear goggles while doing this so the pieces from the casting do not fly into your eyes. Shape the smaller areas with needle files.

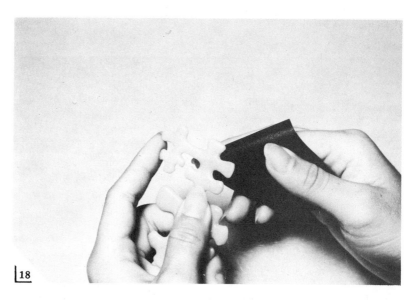

18 Finish off the back and edges of the casting with wet/dry sandpaper in progressively finer grades (180, 220, 340, 420, 500, 600).

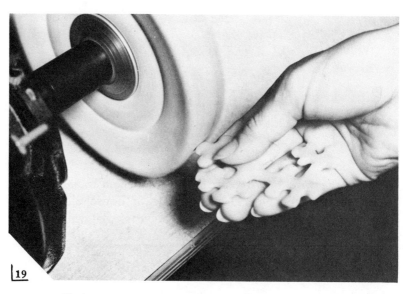

19 Buff the casting with either aluminum oxide compound or tripoli on a center-sewn muslin wheel. Further polishing may be done using a paste wax on a flannel cloth.

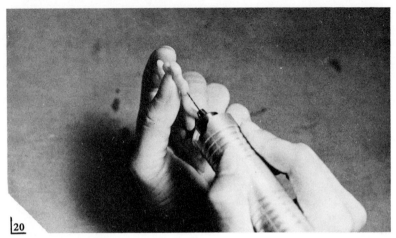

20   Using a flexible shaft with a high speed drill bit, drill holes for wire eyes.

21   Cut the wire eyes to size and attach them to the casting using a casein-type glue. Airplane glue or household cement cannot be used because they contain solvents that will dissolve the acrylic and make the hole larger.

22   Use findings with screw bases because they will stay firmly attached if screwed into the casting. With a highspeed drill in a

22

flexible shaft, bore holes in the back of the casting for the screw-ended findings. Attach the pin stem to the screw base and screw it into place.

23

23 Attach jump rings to join the dangling pieces to the completed pin.

FURTHER SUGGESTIONS

In photograph A, dried parsely was mixed with the clear dental acrylic to give color and interior texture to the casting. Other spices that do not dissolve in water can also be used. In photograph B, a thin layer of acrylic was cast, and the back of that casting was sanded; then acrylic paint was used to

  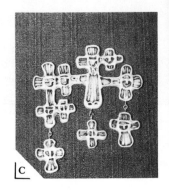

paint a design on the back. It is necessary to sand an area that is to be painted; otherwise, the paint will just puddle and will not adhere to the surface. After painting the back, a layer of acrylic paint may be painted over the design to stabilize it and a final casting of clear acrylic is poured on top of that. In photograph C, a wax-based shoe polish was rubbed into the lowered areas to bring out the design after the piece had been buffed to the desired lustre. A further idea would be to cast one color in the raised areas and another color in the lowered areas.

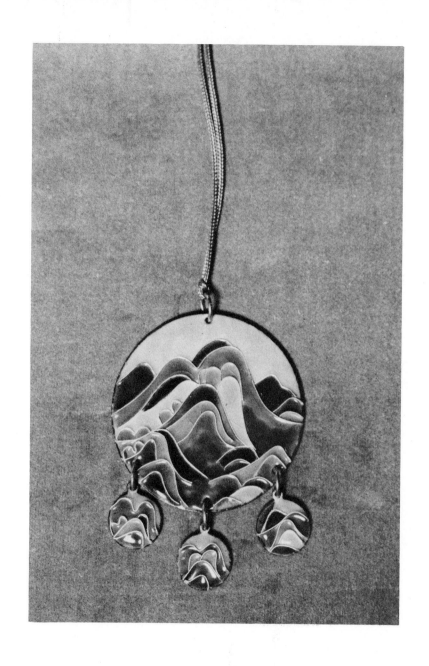

ten

ENAMELING

The enameled pendant on the preceding page, by Martie Rhodes, shows an effective use of cloisons to separate color areas in cloisonné enameling.

Enameling is the process of placing a powdered glass on a metal surface and melting the powdered glass in an enameling kiln at temperatures between 1350° F. and 1550° F. There are many different enameling techniques that can be pursued, such as, *cloisonné, basse taille, champlevé, plique-a-jour, limoges, grisaille,* and *majolica,* but in this chapter the very simple technique of *stenciling* will be presented. In connection with stencil enameling it is necessary to know that different colors of enamel will fire at different temperatures. This means that colors must be used in temperature order with the highest firing color being used first and the lowest firing color being used last. If the order of firing temperature of enamels is not followed, some colors will bubble through others and create spots of the bottom color in the top color or else colors will burn off, leaving black holes in the enamel piece. Reds usually fire at high temperatures, yellows at medium temperatures, and blues and greens at low temperatures. Lower firing enamels are also available. Gold enamel is available at lower firing temperatures and is ideal for adding accents to an enamel piece. An enameling kiln is generally used for firing, but butane torches may also be used. When using a butane torch, the enameled piece is heated from the bottom of the piece so that the enamel is not burned.

An accidental overfiring of the background color of this enameled pendant by Karen Enos heightens the idea of the stenciled flame design.

This stencil enameled pendant by Laurie Miyamoto shows the interesting effect obtained by allowing a few of the enamel grains from the last stenciling to remain in the blocked out areas.

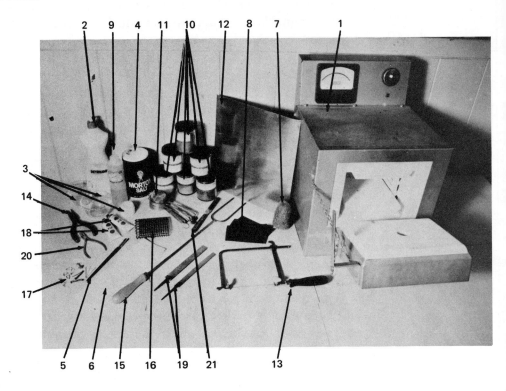

Metals that might be used for enameling are gold, fine silver (sterling silver would melt), copper, and steel. The beauty of using gold and fine silver is that the fire scale (a discoloration or darkening of the metal or burning of the metal caused by exposure to heat or fire) is not as noticeable as when copper is used. Copper will also tarnish faster than gold or silver.

This stenciled pendant by the author repeats the color of the enameling in the pieces of horn, ceramic, and glass beads attached to it.

Supplies	Sources of Supplies*
1. Enameling kiln with a pyrometer	1. AAC, AH, ATS, BAC, BG, CCI, DRH, EH, JLH, MAC, SAC, TAC, TCT, WCS
2. Detergent	
3. Three glass containers	
4. Salt	
5. Two paint brushes	
6. Paper towels	
7. Steel wool	
8. Wet/dry sandpaper	
9. Gum solution (gum tragacanth)	9. AAC, ATS, BAC, CRH, JLH, MAC, SAC, TAC, TCT, WCS
10. Enamels	10. AAC, AH, ATS, BAC, BG, CRH, CWC, EH, JLH, MAC, SAC, SCC, TAC, TCT, WCS
11. Tea strainers	
12. Metal sheet (16 to 18 gauge)	12. AH, ATS, BAC, CRH, EH, MAC, SCC, SI, TAC, WCS
13. Jeweler's saw and blade	13. AH, ATS, BAC, BG, CCI, CRH, JLH, MAC, SAC, SI, TAC, TCT, WCS
14. Wire cutter and plier combination	
15. Enameling fork	15. AAC, AH, ATS, BAC, CRH, EH, MAC, SAC, SCC, TAC, TCT, WCS
16. Wire mesh screen	16. AAC, ATS, BAC, CRH, EH, MAC, SCC, TAC, TCT, WCS
17. Findings	17. AAC, ATS, BAC, BG, CRH, EH, MAC, SCC, SI, TAC, TCT, WCS
18. Jeweler's glue or cement or epoxy	
19. Files	
20. Jeweler's pliers	20. ATS, BAC, BG, CCI, JLH, MAC, SI, TAC, WCS
21. Enameling spatula	21. AAC, ATS, CRH, EH, JLH, SAC, SCP, TAC, TCT, WCS

*Letters refer to mail order outlets listed in *Appendix B: Addresses of Suppliers.*

Enamels are composed of powdered glass. When they are fired, the glass powder fuses together to form a glass surface on the metal. If a piece is dropped, the metal will bend and the glass (enamel) surface will crack and may even chip off. So handle your piece as if it were glass; it is.

When enameling, put thin, but adequate, layers of the powdered enamel on the surface of your metal. If too thin a layer is put on, parts of the metal will be exposed on the surface and will acquire fire scale that must be sanded off. If too thick a layer is put on, the enamel will crack and chip off. If cracks do appear, it is possible to refire the piece, but the crack line will show unless more enamel is put over that area. If your enamel is already too thick, you will need to file the surface down with either a file or a carborundum stone. If you use a carborundum stone, do the stoning under running water.

Thick coats of enamel will cause the metal to become convex on the enameled surface. An enamel piece is kept flat by counter-enameling it on the back side first. However, in small pieces and jewelry pieces that require findings on the back, it is not necessary to counter-enamel the back of the piece.

STENCIL ENAMELING

Creating a Design for Stencil Enameling and Preparing the Metal Piece

1   Make a simple shape for your metal piece. REASON: This will eliminate difficult areas to be filed and sanded. If the shape curves inward, it is more difficult to file than if it curves outward. You may purchase precut metal blanks, if you desire, instead of cutting out your own shape from a sheet of metal. Create a design for your piece that can be cut out of a piece of paper and used to block out areas that will not receive enamel in the second enameling process. Place a sheet of carbon paper

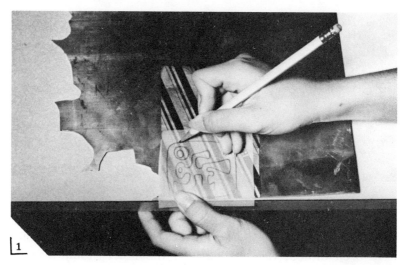

face down on the sheet of metal that is to be cut. Put your design on top of the carbon paper. Trace over the outline of the shape of the metal piece with your pencil. This will leave a carbon outline on the metal.

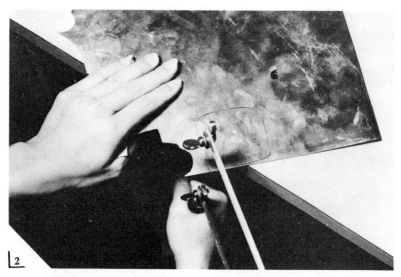

2   Hold the jeweler's saw in a vertical position so that the saw blade is perpendicular to the sheet of metal. REASON: The blade will break if the saw is not held perpendicular to the metal surface. Saw the piece from the metal sheet following the carbon lines that have been drawn. NOTE: Step 2 may be omitted if a precut metal blank is purchased. Drill holes in the piece at this time if they are needed.

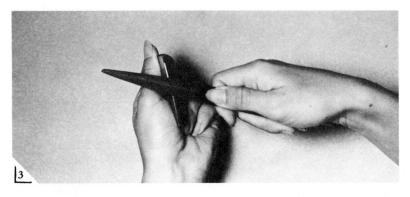

3   File the edges of the piece, keeping the file perpendicular to the surface. Hold the piece in your hand as shown and file the edges at a right angle to the surface of the piece. If holes have been drilled, the burr around the holes should also be removed with a file at this time. Sand the edges, front, and back surfaces with increasingly finer grades of wet/dry sandpaper (180, 220, 340, 420, 500, 600) to remove any and all marks left by the file and any surface scratches. Use steel wool on the front and back surfaces of the piece to restore it to its original high luster. The piece may be further polished using a buffing wheel and jeweler's rouge.

Beginning the First Enameling

4   Wash the metal piece in a solution of detergent and water to remove all the grease and oil from the metal. After washing, rinse in water and dry with a paper towel. Be careful not to touch the surfaces of the metal with your hands. REASON: If grease or oil are on the surface of the metal, the salt water

solution and the gum solution will puddle and will not spread evenly over the piece. If the salt water puddles, some of the fire scale (shown in picture 11) will adhere tenaciously to the metal and will be difficult to remove. If the gum solution does not go on smoothly, the powdered enamel will adhere unevenly to the surface and later will cause areas of the enamel to crack and chip off.

5   Paint a solution of salt water over the back of the piece to be enameled. This will allow the fire scale on the metal to flake off after the firing. Do not allow any of the salt water solution to touch the surface of the metal to be enameled. REASON: If the salt water solution is under the enamel, the enamel will flake off the metal just as the fire scale does.

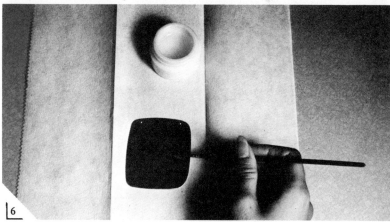

6   After the salt water solution dries, flip the piece over without touching the metal. Paint the gum solution on the front surface.

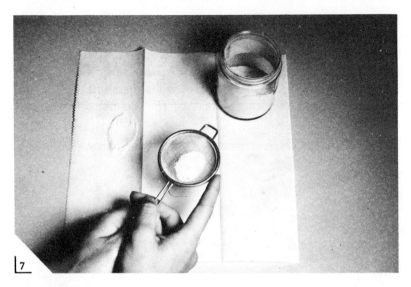

7   Place the powdered enamel in a tea strainer and sprinkle the enamel lightly over the surface of the piece by tapping the strainer with your forefinger. A different tea strainer should be used for each color to keep the colors pure. It is not a good idea to wash the tea strainers because the enamel can become clogged in the holes when it is wet.

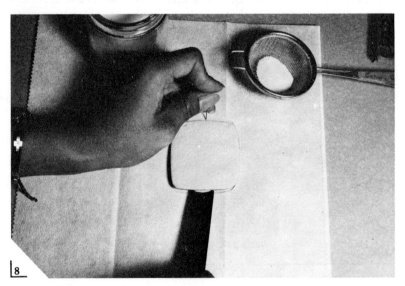

8   Use a pin at the top of the metal piece to stabilize it while slipping a spatula underneath it. Using the spatula, lift the metal piece with the powdered enamel on it onto the metal screen.

9   Clear any holes and the edges of enamel powder by using a straight pin or a probe. REASON: If the holes and edges are cleared of enamel before firing, it will not be necessary to redrill the holes through the enamel or use a file to remove the enamel from the edges after the piece has been fired. Allow the piece to dry on top of the heated kiln. REASON: If the piece is not allowed to dry thoroughly before firing, pits caused by the air in the liquid gum solution may occur on the surface of the enamel during the firing, and they will remain after the firing as black holes in the surface of the enamel.

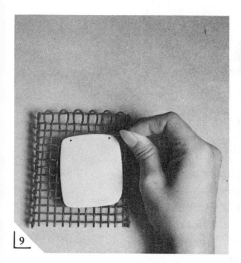

10   Using an enameling fork, place the piece in the kiln. As you watch the piece through the peephole in the kiln, you will notice various changes in the enamel surface. First, the enamel will darken; then, the enamel will become shiny but the surface will be lumpy. When the surface of the enamel is both shiny and smooth, remove the piece from the kiln. Place the piece on top of the kiln and allow it to cool slowly. REASON: Placing the newly enameled piece in a cool area immediately after removing it from the kiln could cause the enamel to crack due to the sudden change in temperature.

11

11   Photo 11 shows fire scale (from the burned salt water), which occured on the back of the enameled piece during the firing process. The salt water solution has acted as a shield to prevent fire scale from building up on and adhering to the metal. It can be easily brushed off. The center section is darker because not enough salt water reached that area. Remove any stubborn fire scale (black areas) using progressively finer grades of wet/dry sandpaper. REASON: If this is not done, the fire scale will flake off and jump up onto the surface of the piece during the next firing process and cause black spots on the surface of the enamel. These cannot be removed without removing some of the enamel in the process. Be sure to sand the edges of the metal as well as the back. Use steel wool on the piece to bring back the original luster of the metal. Instead of sanding the piece, a jeweler's pickling solution can be used to clean the metal surface. The cooled enamel piece is placed in a warm pickling solution to remove the fire scale. The piece may then be steel-wooled to bring back its original luster. This method of cleaning is useful if you do not wish to cover the entire metal surface with enamel at first, but wish to build up overlapping layers of opaque and transparent colors. In preparation for the second firing, repeat steps 4 and 5.

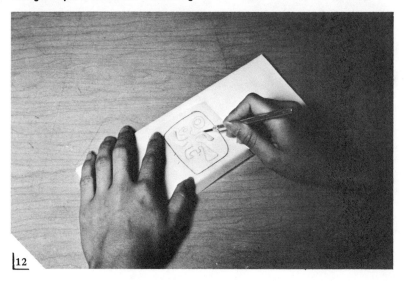

12   Using a stencil cutting knife, cut out the design from the paper (heavy weight tracing paper). Paper towels or newspapers can be used as padding to prevent cutting the surface of the table.

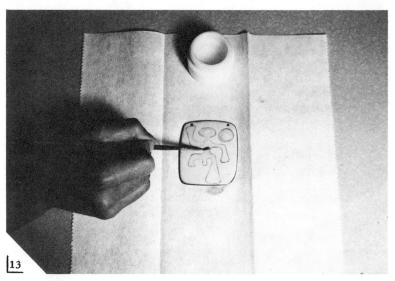

13   Apply the gum solution to the entire surface of the enameled piece. Position the paper frisket. Apply the gum solution to the paper frisket so that the solution soaks through the paper and holds the frisket in place temporarily.

14 Dust the powdered enamel onto the entire surface of the piece.

15 Using a probe, pin, or tweezers lift the paper frisket from the enameled surface.

16 Some grains of the powdered enamel may fall onto areas where they are not desired, but this can be easily corrected. By using a slightly dampened brush dipped in the gum solution or in water, lift off the enamel grains or brush them to the edges of the design. Using a straight pin to stabilize the metal piece, push the spatula underneath it. Using the spatula, lift the piece onto

16

the enameling screen. With a straight pin, clear the holes and edges of unwanted enamel. Allow the piece to dry out on top of the warm kiln. Using an enameling fork, place the piece into the kiln for its second firing.

Finishing the Enameled Piece

17

17   After the piece has been fired, place it on top of the kiln to allow it to cool slowly. Color from the first firing shows through the second layer of enamel for two reasons: (1) the second enamel was not thick enough; (2) the enamel was over-

fired, causing the bottom enamel to bubble through to the surface. Sand the edges and back of the piece with wet/dry sandpaper of progressively finer grades. Use steel wool on the back of the piece to bring back the original luster of the metal. The original luster of the metal can be retained by putting a thin coat of clear nail polish on the back of the piece. Attach jump rings to the piece and add a chain. The finished piece is to be worn as a pendant.

FURTHER SUGGESTIONS

Richly textured surfaces can be obtained by using transparent enamels over opaque enamels, building up white slowly on a black background to create fine value gradations, using colored foils underneath transparent colored enamels, and scratching through areas of powdered enamel to reveal previously enameled colors. You can also apply enamels to stained glass. Any stained glass or glass enamel work should be allowed to cool down inside the kiln to room temperature before removing it from the kiln in order to prevent the glass from shattering with the extreme change in temperature. Enamels can also be sandwiched between pieces of clear glass and fused together in the kiln. Once you have mastered stencil enameling, you will want to explore the traditional methods of enameling mentioned at the beginning of this chapter.

eleven

CERAMICS

The pinch pot by Karen Enos on the preceding page shows a creative exploration of texturing.

Clay is a very pliable substance that can be shaped easily into almost any desired object. Clay has been used for centuries for pots, fetishes, containers, jewelry, sculpture, and architecture. It can be modeled, cut and draped inside and on top of forms, rolled into coils that are joined together, and, when leather hard, it can be carved. Some of the ideas mentioned above will be shown in this chapter.

Not all mud is clay. Clay is obtained from certain clay deposits located throughout the world. It can be obtained in both the moist and dry powder state. If it is obtained in the dry powder state, it must be mixed with water and be allowed to dry and cure on plaster bats before it is used. Once the moist clay has been obtained, it is wedged to remove air bubbles and then formed into the object desired. Leftover clay may be stored in porcelain containers, plastic bags, or plastic containers with tight fitting lids. After a day or two of slow drying, the clay piece reaches a leather hard stage in which it can be trimmed or carved as desired. After further slow drying it is placed in a kiln that has been vented and the kiln is turned on low to allow any remaining moisture to evaporate. After a few

This ceramic vase by Keith Smith is an example of a pinch pot that grew.

Nolan Miguel created this unusual heart-shaped bank using the slab method.

hours (depending on the type of kiln used), the kiln is closed and is allowed to go to the temperature needed to bisque fire your piece. The bisque fire is usually the first firing that the ceramic piece is exposed to. Following the bisque firing, the kiln is allowed to cool down (about 24 hours), and the kiln is cracked (opened slightly). After a few hours, the bisque ware can be removed from the kiln. Glaze is then applied to the bisque ware and the piece is fired at a higher temperature than the bisque firing but only to the necessary firing temperature of the glaze that has been applied. Pyrometric cones that melt at different temperatures are used inside of the kiln to give you some idea as to the interior temperature of the kiln. These are generally used even if your kiln has a pyrometer and an automatic shut-off.

This hanging vase by Karen Enos shows the combination of the slab technique in clay with macramé work.

CLAY BODIES

There are many varieties of clay bodies available to the ceramicist. The type of clay you choose depends on what you desire to create. Some types of clay are discussed below.

Grogged clay: This is a clay body that contains finely ground particles of fired clay called *grog*. During the drying process the grog helps the clay piece to dry more evenly. Grogged clay has the property of good weatherability once it has been fired. For these reasons grogged clay is frequently used in sculpture work.

Earthenware: A type of porous clay body that is usually fired between 1800° F. and 2100° F. (cone 06 to cone 3). This would be considered a low-fire clay. This clay would be good for objects that do not hold liquids.

Stoneware: A type of nonporous clay body that is usually fired between 2100° F. and 2300° F. (cone 3 to cone 9). This is considered a high-fire clay. Stoneware clay can be used for objects designed to hold liquids.

GLAZES

When you purchase clay, it is a good idea to obtain the glaze or glazes you plan to use on your finished piece. You will want to check to be sure that the cone range of your glaze is similar to the cone at which your clay matures. This will insure a proper "fit" of the glaze on the object you are glazing. Purchased glazes come in glossy or matte finish as well as opaque or transparent. The type of glaze you will purchase will depend on the effect you wish to achieve. Glazes may be purchased in both dry and liquid states. Most dry glazes require the addition of water and gum tragacanth. With the help of a ceramic supply house or another ceramicist in the area, you might like to try to create your own glazes with the basic oxides and other chemicals. Glaze formulas are provided in many books on ceramics. CAUTION: If you plan to use your piece for food or drink, make sure that the glaze you use is nontoxic. Check the labels carefully. Lead is a toxic chamical but with the addition of frit, a fused and fired glass compound, the lead can be rendered nontoxic.

If you are glazing a high-fire clay body after a bisque firing, dampen the piece first so that the wetness will help pull the glaze evenly into the clay. Low-fire clay may be glazed before the bisque firing. You can do both the bisque and glaze firing at the same time on low-fire clay.

Lusters may also be purchased, and they are usually of a low firing temperature. These are put on a previously glazed and fired piece and add a decorative touch to the piece.

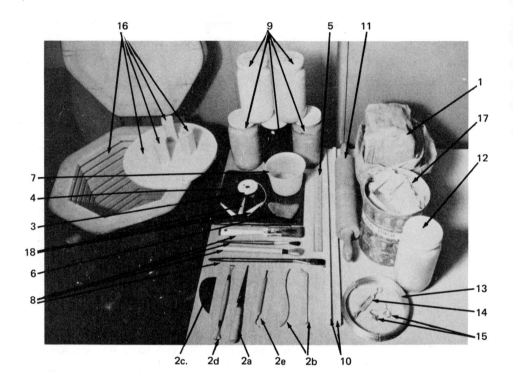

KILNS

Kilns can vary in price from a few hundred dollars on up. You may want to wait to see how you do in ceramics before you purchase your kiln. There are many places that will fire your ceramic pieces for you for a fee: local ceramic shops, community centers, schools, or a local potter or ceramic club.

Many types of kilns may be purchased commercially; however, for home use, the electric kiln is the least expensive and "cleanest" to use. An electrician should be consulted before hooking up the kiln, and a local ceramic firm representative should test the kiln with a kiln setter before you begin to

Supplies	Sources of Supplies*

1. Clay
2. Tools
   a. Fettling knife
   b. Wooden modeling tools
   c. Metal scraper
   d. Wire modeling tools
   e. Sgraffito tool
3. Nylon fishing line or thin
   piece of wire
4. Oilcloth
5. Ruler
6. Elephant ear sponge
7. Dish for water
8. Brushes
9. Glazes
10. $3/8$-inch thick sticks
11. Rolling pin
12. Container of slip
13. Wire for cutting wedged
    clay
14. Turnbuckle for wedging
    wire
15. Screw eye and hook for
    wedging wire
	Consult your Yellow Pages for a listing of ceramic supply houses in your immediate area. Some mail order ceramic supply houses are as follows: AAC, ACC, BAC, BG, CCI, CHL, DCP (no kilns), EH (no kilns), JDW, JLH, KSS, MAC, NPS, SAC, SCC, SCP, SOC, TAC, WCS.

16. Kiln and kiln furniture	16. Many ceramic shops, high schools, and community centers have kilns and will fire your pots for a fee.
17. Kiln wash 18. Pyrometric cones	

*Letters refer to mail order outlets listed in *Appendix B: Addresses of Suppliers.*

operate it. Whether you purchase a low-firing or a high-firing kiln will depend on the type of clay you use and what you desire to create. When you purchase a kiln, you should also purchase *kiln furniture*. Kiln furniture should include whole shelves, a half-shelf or two, kiln posts to support the shelves, and stilts or pins for individual ceramic pieces. Kiln wash in powder or liquid form should also be purchased. Paint the bottom of the kiln and kiln shelves with kiln wash to protect them from glaze drippings during firing. If you are planning on making beads and glazing them, nichrome wire and wire holders might also be purchased. You will need pyrometric cones for bisque and glaze firing.

PYROMETRIC CONES

Pyrometric cones are made of clay that will melt at certain temperatures; they are used by ceramicists when firing clay in order to tell the interior temperature of the kiln. Usually three of these cones are placed in the kiln prior to firing. They are located near the spy hole of the kiln so that they can be watched during the firing process. The cone with the desired firing temperature is placed between two "guard" cones. One guard cone is of a lower firing temperature than desired, and the other is of a higher temperature than the desired firing. The lower firing cone will melt first and when the middle or correct firing temperature cone begins to bend, it is time to turn off the kiln. You will usually need two "sets" of cones. One set will be for the bisque (or first) firing. High fire clay can be bisque fired at cone 016. This helps to solidify the clay and make it less fragile and easier to handle. A second set of cones will be needed for the glaze firing. If your glaze fires at cone 6, then you will need cones 5, 6, and 7 for your glaze firing. Even though a kiln may have an electric timer, it is a good idea to use cones since sometimes timers can go awry. Never fire a kiln according to the length of time it took the last time. Electric current output may vary and considerably change the firing time.

TEXTURING

Aside from the actual fun of creating an object out of clay is the pleasure that can be derived from texturing the surface of the object you create. By texturing you can change the surface quality of the object you have made.

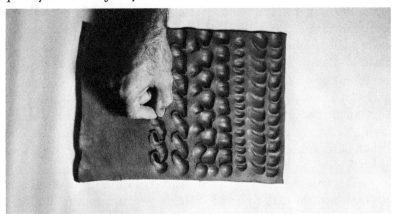

You can hand texture clay by using only your fingers. Push your fingers in and out of the clay at different angles; do a row of each angle. Pinch the clay together using two, three or four fingers; do a row of each. This will create a repeated, rhythmical texture. Continue doing this for each of the experiments that follows. Pull your fingers across the surface of the clay, varying the depth at which you place your fingers. Pinch and twist the clay with your fingers.

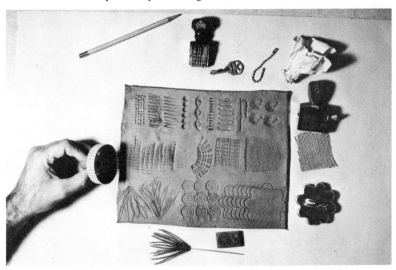

Clay may be textured with tools and other objects. Experiment with a pencil. Put the point into the clay. Pull the point in short strokes across the clay. Lay the sharpened end sideways into the clay. Press the eraser end of the pencil into the clay.

Press the point of a key into the clay. Press the end of the key into the clay. Pull the sides of the key across the clay. Crumble up a piece of paper toweling and press it into the clay. Press burlap into the clay. Use cookie cutters to create repeated patterns. Use rubber stamps to create a texture. Use old type, rubber stamp letters, old typewriter keys, etc. to create textures. Lay natural materials, such as leaves, on the surface, and run a rolling pin over them, and lift them off, leaving the texture of the material behind. This can be used for a single print or repeatedly as a texture over the entire surface. Use other natural materials and press them into the clay in various ways to obtain different textures.

Textures or designs can be carved in plaster of Paris and pressed into the clay to create a single design, a repeated design, or a repeated texture. Carve a plaster cylinder and roll it across the clay. Glue objects to a surface and press that surface into the clay. When the clay is leather hard, scratch, cut, or carve it with sharp objects and knives.

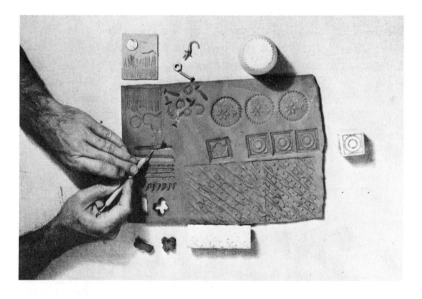

Textures can also be created in clay by adding pieces of clay to the surface of the clay piece. Roll small balls of clay and press and pull them to attach them to the surface of the moist clay. Roll coils of clay and attach them by nicking up the two clay surfaces with a sharp tool (scoring) and joining them together using slip (clay to which water has been added until it has the consistency of thick cream) as you would use glue.

Make small coils of clay into crescents and press them into the clay, one on top of the other, working from the top to the bottom or vice-versa. Roll clay coils into flat spirals and press them into the clay surface. Push the clay through a tea strainer and join the resulting "spaghetti" to a moistened clay surface. Shave moist clay with a razor blade or knife and join it to a moistened clay surface. Many more ideas on texturing will come to you as you look through the kitchen and workshop areas of your home.

WEDGING THE CLAY

Before you create an object from clay, you must *wedge* it to remove the air bubbles and make it of even consistency. If the air bubbles are not removed, the air inside the air bubble will expand when heated in the kiln and fracture the piece. There are different ways of wedging clay. Two methods are given below.

1   In a standing position throw the clay vigorously down on a hard surface. You should hear a snap during this process. This will be the air bubbles breaking. As you wedge the clay, keep it in a rectangular shape. After you have slammed the clay on the hard surface several times, cut it with the wedging wire and

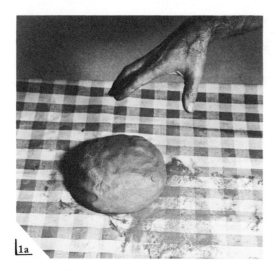

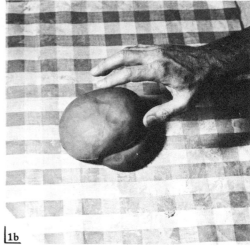

check for air bubbles. If the piece still has air bubbles, as shown in step 3, continue the wedging process. Join the two pieces by throwing one of the cut pieces down on the hard surface and then throwing the other half of the cut piece on top of it with great force.

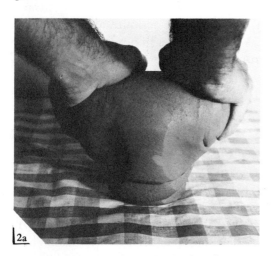

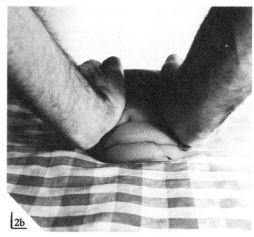

2   In the second method, the clay is kneaded like dough. Lift the clay up from the back and push down and in from the sides in the front. As you work the clay, keep pushing from the outer edges inward with the heel of your hand to keep it compact, otherwise, it will spread out at the sides. This method of rotating and kneading the clay exposes new surface areas of the clay and pushes the air bubbles out that are near the surface of the clay.

3   Cut the clay with the wedging wire to check for air bubbles. This piece shows air bubbles and needs to be wedged some more. You should wedge your clay for about 15 minutes.

4   After wedging the piece a few more times, cut it with the wedging wire to check for air bubbles. This piece is free from air bubbles and will be ready for use after it has been wedged together again.

WORKING THE CLAY

After you have wedged the clay, it may be worked into the object desired. Try to keep the clay piece the same thickness throughout; otherwise, some parts will dry out before others and the piece will crack during the drying or during the firing process. Keep in mind that clay shrinks about ten percent when drying and another ten percent during the firing process.

Below are given three different ways to work clay with a minimum of tools and equipment. All of these projects were done using high-fire clay, but they can easily be done using low-fire clay. The only difference in method would be that if you use the low-fire clay, you can do both the bisque firing and the glaze firing at the same time rather than doing two separate firings.

PINCH POT

Pinch pots are easy to make and have infinite possibilities as toothpick holders, ashtrays, small containers with the addition of a lid, bud vases, condiment holders, and so on. The idea is to work with a ball of clay that fits easily in your hand and get the feel of the clay while attempting to create a piece that has a similar thickness throughout.

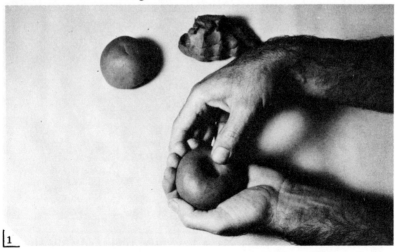

1   Wedge the clay to remove the air bubbles. Then roll the clay into a ball in the palms of your hands. Press your thumb into the center of the ball.

2

2   Work the piece in your hand. Revolve it continually in your hand and press your thumb and fingers against the inside and outside walls of your piece. Use your thumb on the inside against your fingers on the outside to work the clay gradually up to the top.

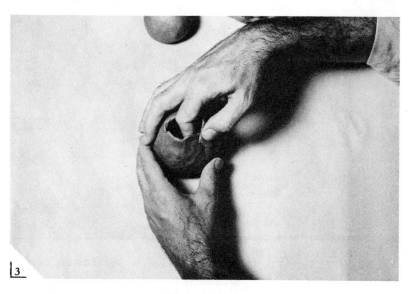

3

3   If you want a narrow opening, overlap the edges. Press these edges together to the same thickness as the body of the pot.

4   Bring the extra clay up into a neck, or cut the extra clay off, leaving a small hole at the top of the pot. Drop the pot lightly on a flat surface to create a stable base for it.

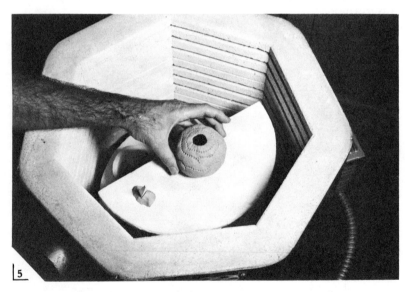

5   Texture the pot, if desired. Allow the "greenware" (clay that has been dried, but not fired) to dry for several days until it is bone dry and has no moisture left in it before placing it in the kiln. Place the bisque fire cone or cones near the spy hole as shown, so they can be conveniently observed during the firing

process. When loading the kiln for a bisque fire, pots may be placed inside of each other. Remove the spy hole stoppers and vent the kiln during the first part of the bisque firing. This allows any chemical moisture left in the clay a chance to escape. For the last part of the bisque firing, follow the firing directions that are in the manual that usually comes with the kiln, because each kiln is different and has different types of setting switches.

6   After the pot has been removed from the kiln, dampen it with a wet sponge and apply the glaze to within ¼ inch of the bottom of the pot. Scrape off any excess glaze that may be on the bottom of the pot so it will not stick to the kiln shelf. Glazed pieces are placed separately in the kiln about 2 inches from the kiln walls and about ½ inch to 1 inch away from each other. Again, place the necessary three cones in front of the spy hole. Remove the spy hole stoppers and vent the kiln to allow any moisture from the glaze to escape during the first part of the glaze firing. Follow the directions in your kiln manual for the last part of the glaze firing.

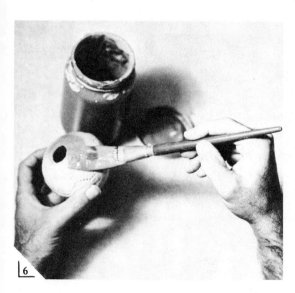 

7   The finished pot is shown here.

SLAB METHOD

Many interesting things can be done with the slab method. Animal shapes can be cut out and draped over newspaper forms or balloons. Boxes and cylinders can be easily formed. Free-form containers, lanterns, sculpture, pendants, and windchimes can be made. Slabs may also be cut and draped in existing bowls or containers. A piece of cloth is usually placed between the two so the clay does not stick to the container.

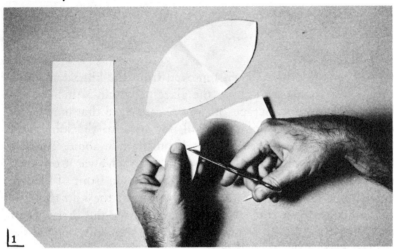

1   Create a design out of paper for your object.

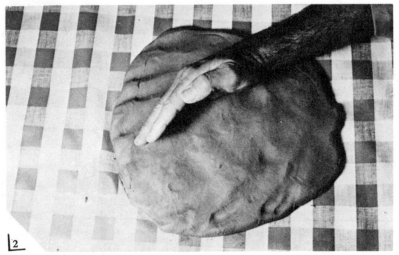

2   Wedge the clay to remove the air bubbles and then flatten the clay by pounding it with the side and flat of your hand.

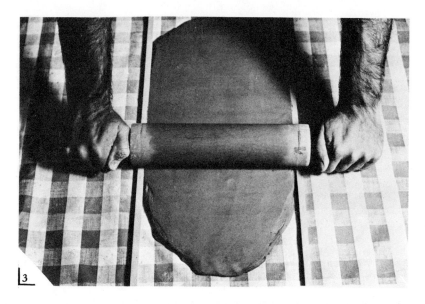

3   Place two sticks, ⅜- to ½-inch thick, on either side of the flattened clay. Roll the clay flat with a rolling pin. Let the rolling pin ride on the top of the two sticks on either side of the clay; this will produce clay of the same thickness throughout.

4   Lay your cut-out paper design on the clay. Using a fettling knife or paring knife, cut out the sections for your project.

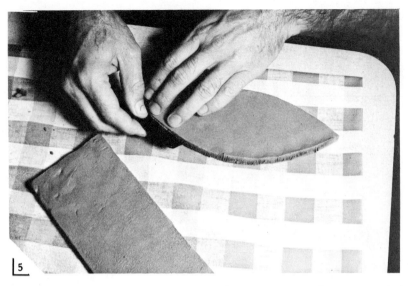

5 Nick up (score) the edges of the sections that are to be joined. A comb is being used here for this process.

6 Mix a thick solution of slip (water and clay) or purchase a container of slip of the same firing temperature and color as the clay you are using. Spread the slip lightly over the scored sections to be joined. The slip needs only to be applied to one of the two pieces to be joined.

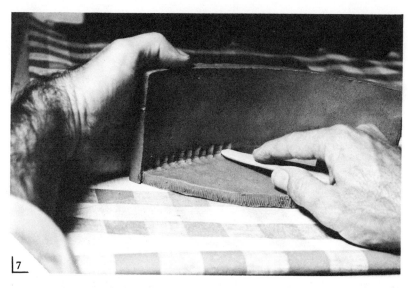

7   Pull the clay back and forth in a tight movement across the joint section to weld the two pieces together. Then, using a wooden ceramic tool, pull the clay down from the walls to join the two pieces together.

8   Wet your fingers with water and smooth the joint, if desired, or use a sponge to smooth over the area. To strengthen the joint, roll a thin strip of clay and apply it to the inside joint section. Work in the rolled strip on the inside using your fingers or a modeling tool.

9 Texture the piece if desired. Support the inside of the pot with your hand, if necessary, while applying the texture.

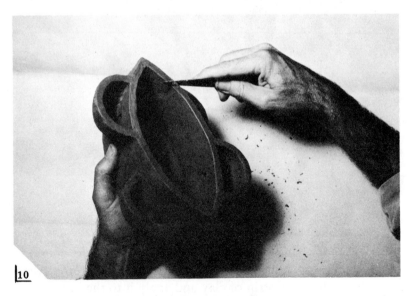

10 After the pot is leather hard, trim away the excess clay using a fettling knife, metal scraper, or sponge.

11 Allow the piece to dry thoroughly. Bisque fire the piece. Dampen it with a wet sponge after the bisque firing, apply the glaze, and glaze fire it. The finished piece is shown here.

COIL METHOD

Coils can be joined together so that they are evident in the finished piece, or they can be smoothed over so that the construction is not evident. The variety of objects that can be made using the coil method is only limited by the craftsman's imagination. Coils can be joined in spirals, woven together, or attached side-by-side to create objects. Creative joining of coils can result in an open design in the finished project, if desired.

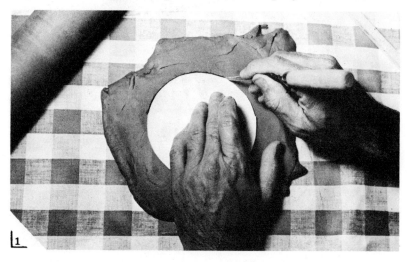

1 Wedge the clay to remove the air bubbles. Flatten out a slab and cut out a piece for the base or make the base out of coils. If you have a hand wheel, place the exact center of the base onto the center of the wheel.

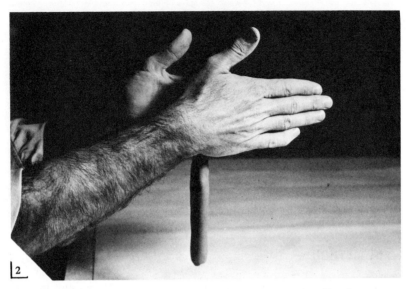

2   To make a coil, take a small ball of clay and roll it between the palms of your hands to form the coil.

3   To make the coil longer and narrower, roll it on a flat surface, working from the center out to the ends of the coil.

4   To join the coils together, score the surfaces of the coils being joined and apply slip to one of the coils or to the surface it is being joined to.

5   Press the coils against each other until they are secured.

6   Allow the piece to dry until it is leather hard and then trim it with a fettling knife or sponge as necessary.

7   Dry thoroughly, and bisque fire the piece. After bisque firing, dampen the piece with a wet sponge and apply the glaze. Glaze fire the piece. The finished piece is shown here.

STORING THE CLAY

Newly purchased clay and clay that has not been used in a project should be stored in a cool, airtight place so that it does not dry out. Clay is usually stored in porcelain crocks made specifically for this purpose; however, a large plastic garbage can with a tight fitting lid is an adequate substitute, as is an old ice box. The ice box does not need to be in working condition; it is only necessary that it have an air-tight seal.

FURTHER SUGGESTIONS

Early texture experiments can be done on ¾-inch thick square tiles that can be used later as hot plates. Cover the tiles with damp paper towels, damp fabric, and plastic sheeting; allow them to dry slowly to prevent warping. Coil and slab techniques can be combined to create interesting projects. Clay rolled out into a slab can be cut into strips and joined in a manner similar to the coil method. The strips can be of varying heights and will provide an interesting surface when joined together. Clay of the same firing temperature but of different colors can be cut and wedged together in checkerboard patterns or in loose flowing patterns. Clay can also be polished using water and your fingers or a smooth stone while the clay is in the greenware stage. The suggestions in this chapter should provide an interesting beginning for further explorations into this medium.

twelve

MOSAICS

The mosaic on the preceding page, by Karen Enos, shows an excellent use of a variety of mosaic materials.

A mosaic is an assemblage of small units into a unified whole. You can see from the definition that the possibilities in this medium are practically infinite. Today mosaics can be anything from plastics, wood, ceramics, and metal to the traditional materials of stone, marble, glass, and tesserae.

Mosaic work can be very satisfying as an individual or group project. You can have great fun in accumulating the necessary colors, shapes, and materials that are to be used in a mosaic piece. It is an activity that can involve one person, a whole family, or a group of people in weekend excursions to the beach, near-by hills, second-hand stores, and junkyards in search of the necessary pieces and colors for the project. Tiles or tesserae can be ordered from catalogues, and this would be an ideal solution if you decide you need a particular color that cannot be obtained in any other way. Although it is time consuming, you can obtain that particular color by enameling copper pieces, glazing ceramic pieces, or painting wood.

Once you have accumulated all your pieces, you might well ask, "What do I want to do with all these pieces?" Well, here again, there are a multitude of things that mosaics can be used for. How about the section of the wall behind your kitchen sink or stove? That wall gets pretty splattered with soap and grease. A mosaic tile wall could be cleaned easily and would add color to the area. Or that outside wall of the garage that

This mosaic by Francis Soberano utilizes beach glass, shells, and pebbles to create a wave.

constantly needs repainting; why not save yourself some work in the long run and put a mosaic on it? That old coffee table out in the garage needs to be refinished; why not put a mosaic on that? That patio needs something, so why not make some mosaic tiles for the ground to add color and beauty to the area? If you are a little hesitant about working on a large project for your first mosaic, how about something small like the lid of a wooden box, a small piece of jewelry, an ashtray, a small picture, or a small sculpture?

This mosaic pendant by Beverly Kahn consists of colored glass that was broken and melted in an enameling kiln until the pieces became spheres; these were glued on a ceramic base designed by Beverly.

Mosaics are easy to do and require very little in the way of materials and equipment. You will need a surface on which to place your mosaics. Three-quarter-inch plywood is suggested for heavy mosaic work in tiles, tesserae, and stone; it will have to support the weight and prevent the warping of the mosaic. An adhesive will be necessary, depending on the type of mosaic materials you use. If you want a transparent effect in your glass work, you will need an adhesive that will dry clear. Stone mosaics require cement or epoxy. You may want to grout your mosaic when you are finished so that the background you used for your mosaic does not show. You can obtain dry colors to mix with the grout to help make the colors of the mosaic stand out better. You might want to use a cold liquid lead around. your glass pieces to help keep the colors separated. If you use

This mosaic by Wendy Stanton was created of pieces of driftwood gathered on the beaches in Hawaii.

tiles or tesserae, you will need a tile nipper to fracture the pieces. If you use glass, a glass cutter might come in handy. You will also need a cartoon (a simple outline drawing) of your project so that you will know where to place your mosaic pieces. Sometimes a small color sketch is helpful in deciding on your color scheme and in figuring out how much tile you will need of the various colors.

There are many different ways to attach the mosaic pieces to a surface. Two ways will be presented in this chapter: the direct and indirect methods. The indirect technique is used when a flat surface such as a table top is desired.

SUPPLIES

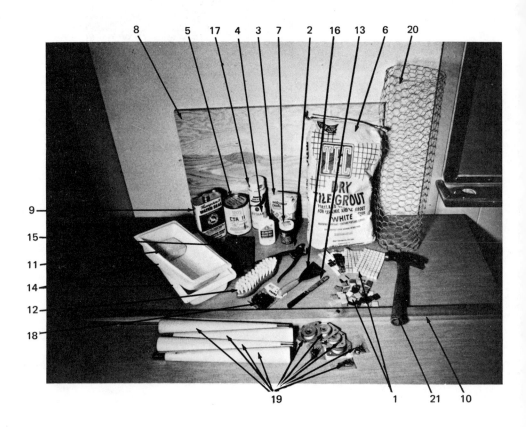

Supplies	Sources of Supplies*
1. Tesserae or tiles	1. AH, DCS (tiles only), EH, MAC, SAC, SCC, TAC
2. Tile nipper	2. AH, BAC, CRH, EH, MAC, SAC, SCC, TAC
3. Water soluble adhesive (e.g., wheat paste) for indirect method	
4. White glue (casein base)	
5. Mastic for indirect method	
6. Grout for direct method	6. AH, BAC, EH, MAC, SCC, TAC
7. Coloring for grout (optional)	7. AH, BAC, EH, MAC, TAC
8. Surface to decorate or ¾-inch plywood	
9. Wood sealer, if using a wood surface	
10. Framing material	
11. Sponge	
12. Scrub brush	
13. Knife or spatula	
14. Disposable mixing containers	
15. Rags	
16. Cement trowel	
17. Waterproofing spray	
18. Tacks	
19. Table legs (if making a table), screws and leg holders	
20. Wire mesh (for large surfaces)	
21. Hammer	
22. Wood putty (not shown)	

*Letters refer to mail order outlets listed in *Appendix B: Addresses of Suppliers.*

DIRECT METHOD

Preparing the Surface

1   To prepare the plywood surface, fill all holes with wood putty and allow it to dry. Coat the plywood with wood sealer when the putty has dried. This prevents the board from warping when the pieces are glued on and the surface is grouted.

2   Prepare a color sketch of your project. If you are using colored tile, this will help you figure out how much colored tile you will need. Sketch your design on the surface with a piece of chalk. Reinforce your design lines with a wide felt tip pen.

3   Attach a frame or edge to your board. Allow the frame to project above the surface of the board enough so that it is ⅛-inch higher than the tiles you plan to glue to the board.

Beginning the Mosaic

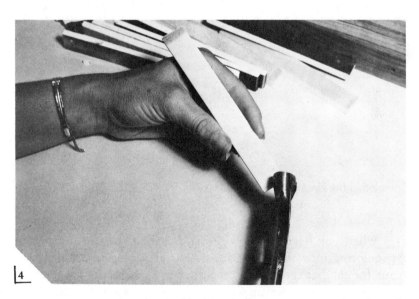

4   When cutting tile, hold the tile between your thumb and forefinger. Place the tile nipper next to the edge of the tile and apply pressure to fracture the tile. It is not necessary to have

the nipper cover the entire line to be cut. Wear goggles when doing this because it is possible that in breaking the tile, a piece could fly into your eye. Cut pieces of tile in various sizes and angles; this will make it easier to assemble your mosaic.

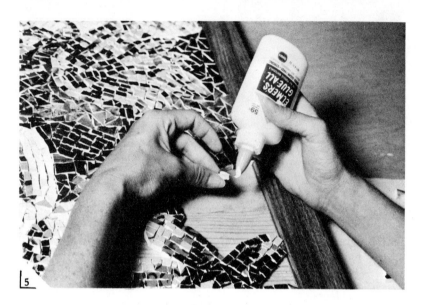

5   Spread white glue on the back of each tile. As you put glue on them, press the tiles onto the board. Follow the contours of your design.

Completing the Mosaic

6   When you have finished gluing down all the tiles, mix the *dry* coloring into the *dry* grout if you are going to color your grout for the background. Remember the proportions you mix so that you can make up another batch later on if necessary. Shift the grout mixture into the water, and mix it to the consistency of cake frosting. Mix only the amount of grout that you can spread and clean off the tiles within a half-hour period.

7   Place the following items near the grout before you start grouting: sponge, dish or pail of water, clean cloth, scrub brush, knife or spatula. Begin grouting at one end of the mosaic. Cover the tiles completely, pushing the grout between the tiles.

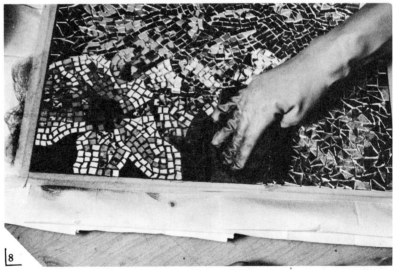

8   When you have used up all the grout you have mixed, take a wet sponge and begin wiping the grout off the surface of the tiles. Clean the sponge in water as you work. Use the scrub brush, knife, or spatula on stubborn areas. If holes appear, use the spatula to apply additional grout to the area. Wipe the area with a dry cloth. Rub the cloth back and forth over the tiles to polish them.

9 After twenty-four hours, spray the piece with a water repellent substance to protect the grout and your mosaic. The completed mosaic project is shown here.

INDIRECT METHOD

Preparing the Design

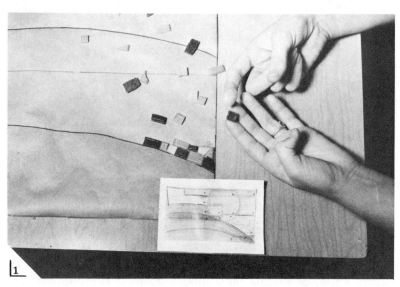

1 Create your design in reverse on a sheet of paper. Using a water soluble glue, such as wheat paste, attach the desired mosaic material upside down to the design on the paper.

2   Cut your backing of ¾-inch plywood to the desired shape. Waterproof the plywood with a wood sealer after you have filled in any existing holes with wood putty. Put the desired edging around the shape. Allow the edging to rise about ½-inch to ¾-inch above the surface of the plywood. Put masking tape on the edging to protect it.

3   Attach the legs, finished in the manner you desire, to the bottom of the table. Nail carpet tacks into the surface of the wood, leaving the heads of the nails raised slightly above the

surface of the wood. This will help to join the plywood and mortar together. For a larger table, nail a wire mesh to the surface and apply two layers of mortar. Using a cement trowel, spread the mortar on the surface of the plywood. CTA-11 is being used here. Cement can be used instead of CTA-11. Wire mesh should be nailed down on the surface of the board, if you use cement, to help the cement adhere to the surface.

Setting the Tiles

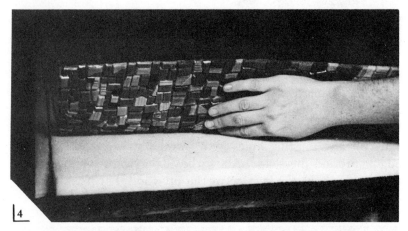

4   Level the mortar with a piece of wood. Place a larger piece of paper, wood, or cardboard over your design and turn the design upside down onto this paper, wood, or cardboard. A piece of discarded packing foam is being used here.

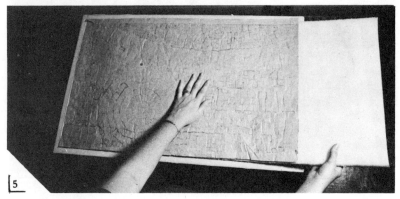

5   Place your design on top of the prepared mortar and position it. Slowly pull out the bottom paper, wood, or cardboard that is between the tiles and the mortar.

6   Press the tiles into the mortar so that they are all level. The piece of wood that you used earlier can be used again to level the tiles. After 4 to 8 hours of setting, wet the back of the paper with a wet sponge and peel the paper off the tiles.

Completing the Piece

7   Clean the tiles carefully so that they are not pushed further into the mortar. Scrub off the excess mortar with scouring pads or scrub brushes, and scrape areas with a knife where needed.

8

8   Coat the surface with a waterproofing substance. The table here is ready for use.

FURTHER SUGGESTIONS

Once you become involved in mosaics you may want to cover a wall or a floor. It is suggested that you hire professional tile setters to assist you with large scale projects. In preparation for this, you can glue your tiles on paper on which you have drawn your design in reverse. It is a good idea to have this paper cut into small units of about 12 by 12 inches to allow for easy handling of the tiles. Another suggestion is that you number each of these units on the back and have a key that the tile setters can go by. Such work is usually done by the indirect method that was just described above.

You can make your own mosaic materials. Try making ceramic pieces. Experiment with textures as well as glazes on these ceramic pieces. Break stained glass into small pieces and melt them in an enameling kiln. In preparation for this, be sure that the kiln shelf has at least two coatings of kiln wash and a coating of whiting (powdered). Mica sheeting can be used as a backing for the glass you wish to melt, since it can easily be peeled off. Leave the glass in the kiln until the kiln has reached room temperature (about 24 hours); the glass will shatter if it is taken out of the hot kiln into the cold air. Glass will melt between 1500° F. and 1750° F. and should be watched carefully through the peephole in the kiln. The small pieces of stained glass will become spherical during this time, while the large pieces will appear to shrink and become rounded on the edges.

There are many different mortars that you can use for the indirect method; there are several good books on mosaics listed in the bibliography that will give you formulas for mortars. Call your local building supply house for information as to what is available for the type of mosaic you are planning to do.

thirteen

LEATHERCRAFT

The leather box shown on the preceding page, by Tracy Doolittle, was a single piece of leather that was then laced together to form the sides and top of the box.

The natural beauty and the ease of working leather makes it a very popular craft. Leather can be obtained in many different forms and sizes from leathercraft catalogues and stores. A wide variety of projects are available, ranging from simple beginner's kits to hides that you can cut to your own patterns. With leather and a few tools, you can create inexpensive and long-lasting projects. Leather purses, billfolds, keycases, and belts are only a few of the beginning projects that you can create at nearly half the cost of mass-produced pieces that do not have the individuality of hand made leather projects.

This simple hair ornament by the author would be an ideal project on which the beginner can learn the technique of either tooling or carving.

As a beginner, you may find that a kit is easier to handle than creating your own patterns, since everything is designed and prepunched so that it all fits together. Once you have acquired the necessary leathercraft skills, you will find it more enjoyable to design and cut your own leather projects. Leather may be purchased from leathercraft catalogues or leathercraft shops as either precut pieces or as whole, half, or side skins. Leather varies in weight and texture as well as size, so you should decide (1) what you will make, and (2) whether you will tool, carve, or leave the surface of your project plain. There are many different types of leather available:

- *Calfskin* is used as a tooling and carving leather, and because it varies from light to medium weight it is used for small, lightweight projects.
- *Cowhide* is ideal for carving as well as tooling and may be used in all types of projects because it varies in weight from light to heavy. It can be used in projects such as lineman's belts that require a heavy weight leather.
- *Pigskin* may be tooled and it comes in various weights.
- *Sheepskin* may be tooled and comes only in a medium weight.
- *Woolskin*, from lambs, makes an excellent soft furry lining for coats, jackets, or after-skiing boots. Since it is skin with animal's hair left on it, it is not used for tooling or carving.

- *Suede* is a finish usually found on sheepskin and it comes in a variety of colors. It can be used for lining, clothes, pillows, bags, and so on. Due to the finish, it is not usually used for tooling.
- *Lizard skins* are small (up to 10 inches in width), but provide an unusual textured surface for small objects such as key cases or wallets on which you do not wish to do any tooling.

There are many more varieties of leather available, and if you look at a leather catalogue or visit a leathercraft shop, you will find a variety of leathers that will keep you busy for some time with creative projects.

This wallet by the author shows the use of a metal stamp to create a textured background for the tooled design.

Besides deciding on whether you will purchase precut leather pieces or skins, you will need to decide whether you want the back, belly, shoulder or bend of the skin if you decide to purchase a skin. The back is the best for carving and tooling; however, the bend and shoulder are contained in the back and therefore are of the same quality as the back. The belly and leg portions of the skin will prove excellent for linings and gussets in billfolds and purses. Skins are usually sold and measured by the square foot, but it is much better to purchase the piece based on quality than on size. Often a leathercraft outlet will not have an exact size but they will send you the size nearest to it, so it is better to insist on the quality you want rather than the size.

Although most of the necessary tools are shown in the supply photograph that follows, a basic explanation of what some of them are and how they are used is necessary.

- A modeling tool or modeler has a narrow pointed end that is used for tracing or tooling designs in leather, and it also has a flat, spoon-shaped end for modeling, or raising or lowering design areas.

- The rawhide mallet has a head made of leather that has been wrapped in a tight cylinder and is used for flattening lacing, setting snaps, and hitting metal stamp designs on leather surfaces.

- A revolving leather punch has cylinders (drive tubes) of various sizes for punching holes for lacing or snaps or rivets.

- A spacer or space marker is a revolving disc of points that marks dots on the leather for sewing or for holes to be punched for lacing.

- The skife (skiver) is a tool containing a razor blade that is used for thinning leather along the edges where the leather is to be sewn or laced. It is used to reduce the thickness of leather to make it more pliable.

LACING

Lacings are leather strips used for joining pieces of leather together. Purchase lacing that is the correct width for the holes you have punched. Lacing that is $\frac{3}{32}$ inch wide will work very well with a $\frac{1}{8}$-inch hole. Strips of leather that are as wide as $\frac{5}{32}$ inch or $\frac{3}{16}$ inch would need larger holes and would be used on larger projects with heavy weight leather.

Always keep the lacing flat, with the rough side next to the leather and the smooth side facing out. Try to avoid twisting the lacing. The three basic stitches used in lacing are the Whipstitch, the Single Cordovan Stitch (Single Buttonhole Stitch), and the Double Cordovan Stitch (Double Buttonhole Stitch).

SUPPLIES

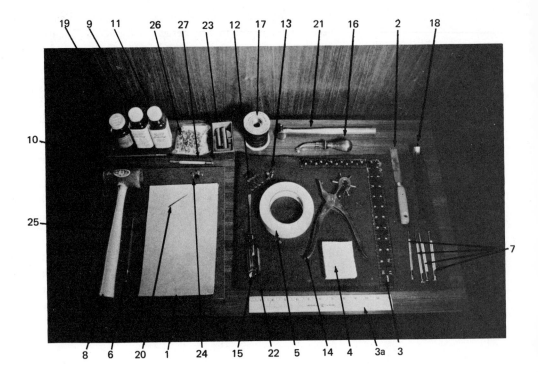

If you purchase a precut and punched leather kit, you may only need a modeling tool, sponge, masking tape, lacing, ¼-inch masonite, skiver, and lacing needle. The supplies listed here are for designing your own key case and would vary depending on what you are making.

Whipstitch

1   For the Whipstitch, put the lacing through the hole from the back. Leave about a 2-inch tail.

214 LEATHERCRAFT

Supplies	Sources of Supplies*
1. Leather	1. BLC, MAC, MSC, SAC, TAC, TLC
2. Sharp knife	2. BG, BLC, EH, MSC, TAC, TLC
3. Steel square or 3A. Metal-edged ruler	3. MAC, TLC
4. Small sponge	
5. Masking tape	
6. Leather modeling tool (Universal Modeler)	6. BG, MAC, MSC, TAC, TLC
7. Metal stamps (optional)	7. MAC, MSC, TAC, TLC
8. Rawhide mallet	8. BLC, GG, MAC, MSC, SAC, TAC, TLC
9. Leather dye (optional)	9. BLC, MAC, MSC, TLC
10. Paint brush (optional)	
11. Leather finish (Carnauba Cream, leather finishing compounds, clear shoe polish, etc.)	11. BG, BLC, MAC, MSC, TLC
12. Key plate (for key case)	12. HBM, MAC, SAC, TAC, TLC
13. Key posts (for key case)	13. HBM, MAC, SAC, TLC
14. Revolving leather punch	14. BG, BLC, EH, MAC, MSC, TAC, TLC
15. Screwdriver (for key posts)	
16. Spacer (five points per inch)	16. BG, MAC, TAC, TLC
17. Lacing ($^3/_{32}$ inch)	17. BG, BLC, MAC, SAC, TAC, TLC
18. Skife (skiver)	18. BLC, EH, MAC, MSC, TAC, TLC
19. Rubber cement	
20. Lacing needle	20. BG, MAC, MSC, SAC, TAC, TLC
21. Small hammer	
22. Felt	
23. Snap setter	23. MAC, SAC, TAC, TLC
24. Snaps	24. BG, MAC, SAC, TAC, TLC
25. Sheet of masonite (¼-inch)	
26. Rivets	26. MAC, SAC, TAC
27. Rivet setter	27. MAC, SAC, TAC

*Letters refer to mail order outlets listed in *Appendix B: Addresses of Suppliers.*

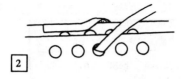

2   Place the 2-inch tail between the two pieces of leather that are being joined together. Place the tail above and between the punched holes and the edge of the piece.

3   Take the long end and go over the top of the edge and behind the piece and through the next hole to your right.

4   When you reach the corner hole, make two or three stitches through it.

BACK SIDE
OR
INSIDE

5   When you reach the end, tuck the end under the lacing on the inside or back of the piece, or put the end between the two pieces of leather that are being joined together.

216 LEATHERCRAFT

Single Cordovan Stitch

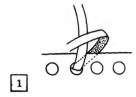

1   Thread the needle with the lacing and go through the punched hole from the front side, then bring the needle forward. (Shaded areas indicate the rough side of the lacing.)

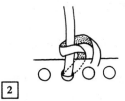

2   Wrap the lacing around the beginning end from the back to the front, around the back of the lacing, and bring the end forward.

3   Go through the next hole from the front and pull the lacing through.

4   Put the needle under the previous stitch toward the back. Continue this process of going through a hole and then making an X by going underneath the previous stitch. When you reach a corner hole, make two or three complete stitches in the same hole before going on to the next hole.

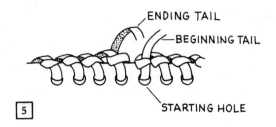

5

5   Finish lacing up to and including the last hole.

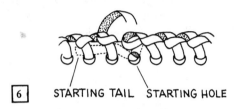

6

6   Pull the starting tail out of the loop and starting hole. Retain the loop. Tuck the starting tail under the first two stitches on the back side, keeping the smooth side of the lacing up and leaving a loop open from the first stitch.

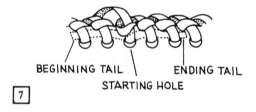

7

7   Put the ending tail through the loop from the top and through the starting hole. Tuck the ending tail under the last two stitches on the back. Tighten the last stitch by pulling the ending tail tightly. Cut off the excess lacing.

Double Cordovan Stitch

1

1   Go through the punched hole from the front, leaving a 2-inch tail. Bring the needle end forward.

218 LEATHERCRAFT

2

2   Wrap the lacing around the beginning end from the back to the front, around the back of the lacing, and bring the end forward.

3

3   Put the needle through the next hole and bring the needle forward.

4

4   Place the end under the X formed by the previous stitch. This will make a 6-pointed star shape (*). Continue this process of going through a hole and then going under the X. When you reach a corner, make two or three complete stiches in the same hole on the corner.

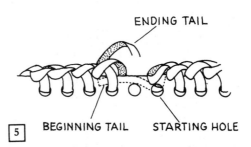

5

5   Complete the lacing until one hole remains. Pull the beginning tail out of the loop and the beginning hole retaining the loop.

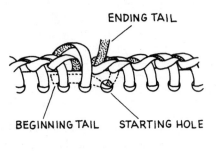

ENDING TAIL

BEGINNING TAIL   STARTING HOLE

6

6   Tuck the beginning tail under the two stitches on the back. Put the needle through the next hole and up through the loop of the first stitch.

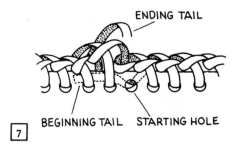

ENDING TAIL

BEGINNING TAIL   STARTING HOLE

7

7   Go back under the X to form a star shape and then prepare to go into the loop of the beginning stitch.

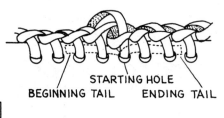

STARTING HOLE
BEGINNING TAIL   ENDING TAIL

8

8   Go down through the loop of the beginning stitch and through the beginning hole from the front and then tuck the ending tail under the last two stitches on the back side, pulling the tail to tighten the stitch. Cut off the extra lacing.

PROCEDURE

Cutting the Leather

1 Draw the shapes of the object on a piece of paper. Cut out the shapes from the paper and check to be certain that the parts fit together correctly.

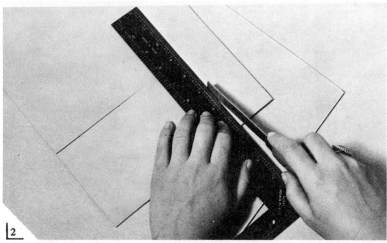

2 Trace the paper pattern onto the smooth side of the leather using the pointed end of the modeling tool, with the curved end flat against the leather. With a sharp knife and a steel square or metal-edged ruler, cut out the necessary leather shapes. Use a piece of ¼-inch masonite under the leather while cutting it. Precut leather kits for various projects can be purchased so that steps 1 and 2 could be omitted.

3   Create the design on a sheet of paper. Take care that no parallel lines are closers than ⅛-inch together because when one of the lines is pressed down, the other will vanish. Using a small sponge or dampened piece of cotton, lightly dampen the back side (rough) of the leather and then dampen the front side (smooth).

4   Attach the design to the leather with masking tape, making certain that the tape is attached to the back side of the leather and does not touch the smooth surface. With the pointed end of a leather modeling tool, keeping the curved end flat against the design, go over the outlines of your design.

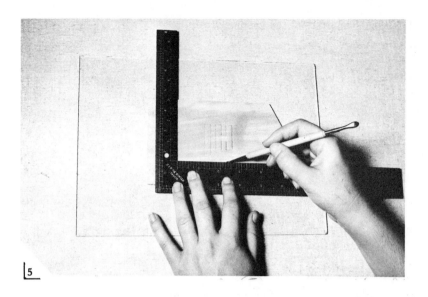

5   Remove the tape and paper design carefully. Using the pointed end of the leather modeling tool, and holding it in the position mentioned before, go over the design.

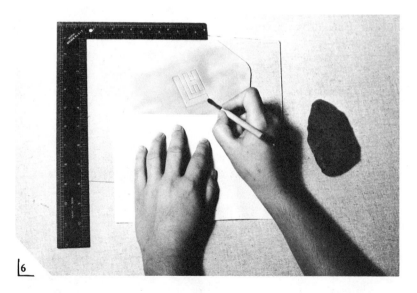

6   To depress areas in the design, use the spoon-shaped end of the modeling tool. Dampen the leather as needed. Texture certain areas, if desired, by using a metal stamp and hitting the stamp with a rawhide mallet.

Finishing the Surface of the Leather

7   Color the desired areas with the leather dye, using a pointed brush. If the entire piece is to be dyed, apply a waterproof dye with a sponge over the entire surface, making certain that the edges and punched holes are also dyed. Wear rubber or plastic gloves while applying the dye. After the dye has dried, apply a leather finish and polish the surface of the piece. There are different types of finishes that can be used for leather: Carnauba cream, leather finishing compounds, clear shoe polish, etc.

Punching the Holes

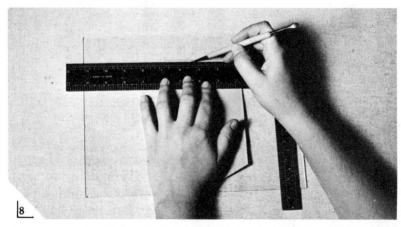

8   Using a ruler and the point of the leather modeling tool, indicate points that are $\frac{3}{16}$ -inch in from the edge of the piece.

With the pointed end of the modeling tool and a ruler, draw a line connecting the points. Next, place the rule on the drawn line so that the $\frac{3}{16}$-inch edge is exposed, and, starting at a corner, roll the spacer along the line drawn with the modeling tool. This will indicate where you will punch the holes in the leather. Use a spacer that marks five points per inch.

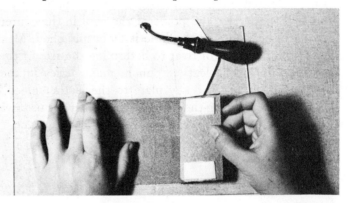

9   Temporarily attach the leather insert piece to the inside of the tooled piece with rubber cement or double-faced tape or a piece of masking tape that has been made into a loop with the adhesive side facing out. Place the tape along the edges that are to be punched.

10   First, punch $\frac{1}{8}$-inch holes on the 4 or 5 corners of the piece. Next, begin punching the leather by working inward from the corners, adjusting the position of the holes where necessary. Remove the tape when all the holes have been punched.

11   Lay the key plate on the leather insert piece at least ½-inch below the top edge. Be sure the key loops are at the top of the leather piece. Place a key in one of the hooks to help locate the position desired for the key plate. Using the point of the leather modeling tool, press the point of the tool in the center of each hole to indicate where the hole is to be punched. Measure the size of the key post or rivet to determine the size of the hole to be punched. With a leather punch, make holes in the leather insert piece. Attach the key plate to the leather piece with the key posts by screwing the key posts together, or use rivets and a rivet setter to attach the key plate to the leather piece.

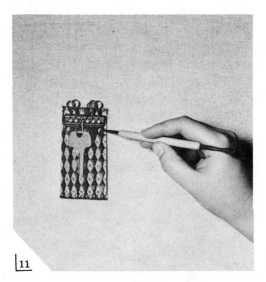

11

12

Setting the Snap

12   Measure the size of the snap by punching various sized holes in a piece of scrap leather. Try the snap in the various holes to determine which size hole will be the best to use. To determine the placement of the snap, place the cap on the top section in the position desired and press the cap lightly into the leather. This will mark the location for the hole. Punch the hole in the top flap section of the piece.

13 Close the key case and, using the pointed end of the
leather modeling tool, mark the position for the bottom half of
the snap. Punch the hole the correct size for the bottom part of
the snap. Follow the directions for setting the snap that come
with the snap setter.

Lacing the Piece

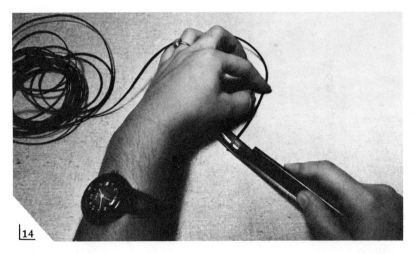

14 To lace the piece, measure the lacing you will need based
on the lacing stitch you plan to use: four times around the edge
to be laced for the Whipstitch, six times around the edge for the
Single Cordovan, and eight times around the edge for the
Double Cordovan. Skive the end of the lacing using a skiver.

15   Open the lacing needle and place the skived end of the lacing between the split ends and parallel to the length of the needle.

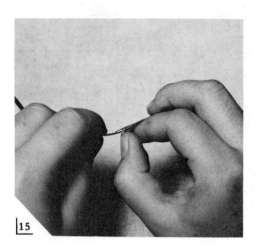

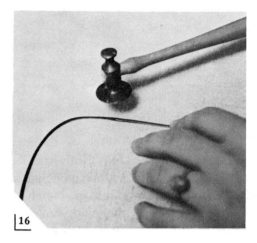

16   Using a small hammer, tap the end of the needle so that the prongs of the needle end pierce the leather lacing. Begin lacing, using the stitch you have chosen.

17   When you have completed the lacing, flatten the lacing by placing the project between two pieces of felt and pound the edges of the piece using a rawhide mallet.

18   The finished key case is shown here.

FURTHER SUGGESTIONS

You could create leather wall hangings made of large sheets of leather, tooled, carved, and painted. Interesting leather pillows could be very durable. A variety of colored suedes could be stitched onto leather or stitched to each other to create pillows or modern wall hangings. Delightful stuffed dolls and animals can be created with leather and will survive any child's rough handling. Leather is also great to use in creating sculptures, jewelry, clothes, hair ornaments, and hats.

Peruvian craftsmen use a technique of raising the surface of leather by placing it over dampened mounds of paper and cotton. The leather is then further dampened and tooled. It is continuously stretched over these dampened mounds until the leather has large raised sections and deep, lowered sections. The paper and cotton mounds eventually dry and are kept permanently in place by sewing a backing onto the tooled piece. This idea can be used to develop sculptural pieces.

In a leather factory in Florence, Italy, leather workers apply gold leaf to the leather surface. The leather is first dampened with water and then a thin film of egg white and oil of lavender or poppy seed oil is applied to the leather. A thin film of gold leaf is lifted up and laid down on the leather with a 3-inch wide short (1½-inch) camel hair brush. An embossing iron is heated and cooled and pressed down on the gold leaf. The extra gold leaf is removed with a wad of cotton that is later burned to reclaim the excess gold leaf.

Leather bags from Morocco use colored narrow strips of leather lacing to create embroidery-like work on the surface of the leather. Strips of colored leather can also be used in weaving projects or to create containers. Leathercraft work has many possibilities, and, once you begin working with it, new ideas will come to mind.

fourteen

STAINED GLASS

The creative night light of stained glass shown on the preceding page, by Marquis Miyauchi, shows one of the possibilities of stained glass.

Stained glass is obtained by mixing chemical oxides (which become a color) with the other powdered chemicals for glass and melting them together. It can be obtained in a variety of forms, as will be explained below. For centuries stained glass has been set in lead (cames) and used for windows in churches. Today, because of the many varieties of stained glass, many different projects can be made with it. If texture or lines are painted on the glass with special chemicals, they can be adhered to the glass by heat. The basic idea in working with stained glass is to take advantage of its translucent quality and brilliant color.

TYPES OF STAINED GLASS

This is a simple project to acquaint the beginner with the techniques of cutting glass, soldering, and using low fire enamel to create or block out an image. Projects created can be used for pendants, shade pulls, or Christmas tree ornaments.

Some of the many different types of stained glass are: *antique glass, cathedral glass, flashed glass,* and *slab glass* (dalles) or *faceted glass.*

- Antique glass is stained glass that has been blown into a cylinder, which is then cut in half and allowed to flatten out into a sheet in a heated kiln. The beauty of this glass is in its variation in color value and the tiny air bubbles that create an interior texture in the glass, causing it to sparkle with light.
- Cathedral glass is a textured sheet of stained glass that has been rolled between metal cylinders (one of which has a textured surface) while the glass is still molten. It is usually cut on the smooth side rather than the textured side of the glass.
- Flashed glass has color on one or both sides of the glass, but the glass in the middle is either clear or a light color. You can see this if you hold the glass up to the light and look through the edge of it. Flashed glass is not recommended for pieces that will have lines or textures painted on them because the surface color will creep back from the edges during the firing process, leaving a clear edge; however, areas of color may be etched so that the surface color of the glass is removed, revealing the interior color of the glass. When this glass is cut, it is best to cut it on the uncolored side, if there is one, to avoid chipping the color off.
- Slab glass (dalles) is stained glass that varies in thickness from ½ to 2 or more inches. This glass must be cut with a double-edged hammer and then further chipped or faceted, a process that causes this type of glass to be referred to as faceted glass. Slab glass is usually set in epoxy or in concrete.

FIRING STAINED GLASS

At times a design for a window will call for detail that can only be painted on. Special low-firing enamels (powdered glass) are mixed with gum tragacanth or an oil, such as oil of lavender or poppyseed oil, and this is painted on the surface of the stained glass. The enamel and gum solution are mixed with a spatula on a nonporous surface, such as glass. These low-firing enamels will fuse to the surface of the glass at about 1050° F. Glass will melt between 1500° F. and 1750° F., so a close watch on the kiln is recommended. A kiln with a peephole or a pyrometer is recommended for this type of work. The kiln shelf should be dusted with whiting or talc (calcium carbonate) before the glass is placed on it so that in the event the glass melts, it can be easily removed from the kiln shelf. The glass should be placed in a cold kiln, and the kiln should be brought up slowly to the desired temperature. It is best to use an enameling kiln that has a temperature control unit so that it can be set at a low temperature for an hour, then at a medium temperature for another hour, and finally at a high temperature until the enamel has melted into the glass. After the enamel has fused with the glass (it will become shiny or disappear into the glass), the kiln

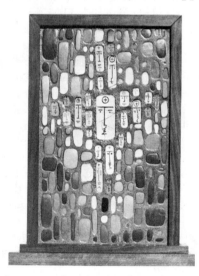 

In "The Mystical Body" by the author, stained glass and copper enameled pieces were cast in epoxy containing a filler. The glass was sandwiched between oil clay during the casting procedure and later removed after the epoxy had cured.

In the abstract of "Saint Francis and the Birds" by the author, a variety of stained glass materials were cast in polyester resin and placed in an open frame to retain the translucency of the stained glass.

is turned off and the glass is left in the kiln until the kiln reaches room temperature, usually a twenty-four hour period. If the glass is removed immediately from the kiln, the extreme contrast in temperature will cause the glass to shatter.

LEAD CAMES

Lead cames are placed around the cut stained glass pieces to hold the pieces to each other. They are either H-shaped, with channels on both sides for interior work, or U-shaped, with a channel on one side for use along the outer edges of the window. The lead came is usually stretched to straighten it out, but enough flexibility should be left so that corners can be rounded. The cames are cut a little shorter than the piece of glass so that the next lead came can overlap the edge of the glass of the previous came. The lead cames are soldered on both sides. A propane torch (Bernzomatic torch) or an electric soldering iron or electronic soldering iron can be used. Resin core solders are not recommended for stained glass work because they are difficult to clean. A solid core wire solder of 60 percent tin and 40 percent lead is recommended for soldering the lead cames. The leads are much too soft to hold the glass, and a specially prepared glass putty must be forced between the leads and the stained glass on both sides to help support the glass. Sometimes cement is used instead of the glass putty. It is often necessary in large work to attach a steel or an iron rod across the window for added support.

SUPPLIES

Supplies	Sources of Supplies*
1. Heavy paper	1. SGC
2. Lead cames (H- and U-shaped)	2. AH, ATS, BAC, EH, MAC, SGC, TAC, WDG
3. Stained glass	3. AH, ATS, BAC, BGC, EH, MAC, SGC, TAC, WDG
4. Cartoon scissors (Pattern scissors) or 4A. Safety razor blade or 4B Scissors	4. SC, SGC, WDG

*Letters refer to mail order outlets listed in *Appendix B: Addresses of Suppliers.*

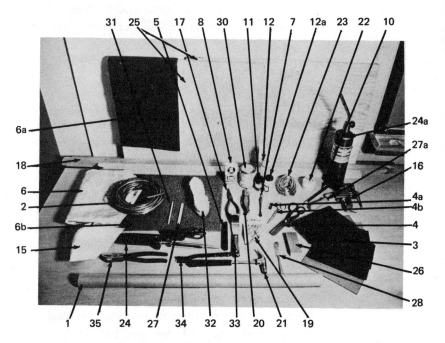

Supplies	Sources of Supplies*
5. Flat felt tipped pen	
6. Newspapers or	
6A. Felt or cutting mat or	6A. WDG
6B. Thick piece of carpet	
7. Glass cutter	7. AH, ATS, BAC, BG, SGC, TAC, WCS, WDG
8. Oil (Three in One) or	
8A. Kerosene (not shown)	
9. Glass circle cutter—Optional (not shown)	9. ATS, BAC, SC, SGC, WCS
10. Grease crayon	
11. Low-fire glass decorating powder enamel (brown or black)	11. AAC, SGC, TCT, WDG
12. Gum tragacanth or	12. AAC, ATS, BAC, CRH, JLH, MAC, SAC, TAC TAC, WCS

Supplies	Sources of Supplies*
12A. Enameling Oil	12A. ATS, BAC, TCT, WCS
13. Enameling kiln (not shown)	13. AAC, AH, ATS, EH, JDW, MAC, SAC, TAC
14. Kiln shelf (not shown)	14. AAC, ATS
15. Whiting, talc, or cleaning and polishing powder	15. ATS, SGC, WCS
16. Vise	
17. Pair of pliers	
18. Strips of wood	
19. Leading nails	19. SC, SGC
20. Sharp knife (for cutting lead cames)	20. SC, SGC, WDG
21. Small claw hammer	
22. Oleic acid flux	22. AAC, ATS, BAC, SGC, WCS, WDG
23. 60/40 soldering wire (nonresin core)	23. BAC, BG, SGC, WDG
24. Electric or electronic soldering iron or	24. AH, BAC, BG, CRH, SGC, TAC, WDG
24A. Propane torch (Bernzomatic torch)	24A. BG, TAC, TCT, WCS
25. Two pieces of plywood or masonite larger than your design	
26. Small block of wood	
27. Tongue depressor or popsicle stick or	
27A. Lathkin	27A. SGC
28. Small flat knife	
29. Steel rods—Optional (not shown)	
30. Stained glass putty	30. ATS, DI, SGC, WDG
31. Orange stick or pointed stick	
32. Scrub brush	
33. Putty knife	33. SGC
34. Wire brush	
35. Glass breaking pliers—Optional	

*Letters refer to mail order outlets listed in *Appendix B: Addresses of Suppliers.*

PROCEDURE

Preparing a Pattern for Stained Glass

1   Create a design on paper. To avoid heavy dark areas and strain on the lead cames, try to have no more than three lines meeting at any one point in your design. Indicate on the cartoon the areas that are to be painted with glass paint.

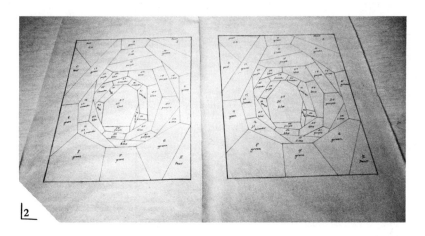

2   Number each section that is to be cut out. Indicate the color of glass that each piece will be. Make a second copy of your numbered design.

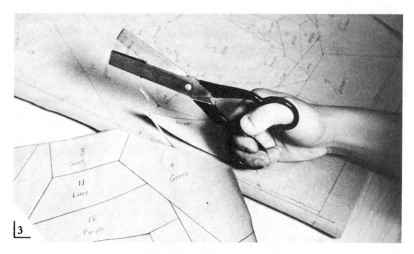

3 Cut out the outside edge of your pattern with a regular scissors, then, using a cartoon scissors (a double bladed scissors that cuts out a $\frac{1}{16}$-inch strip of paper to provide for the lead came) cut out each numbered section from the design. If a cartoon scissors is not available, use a safety razor blade or a pair of scissors to cut out the $\frac{1}{16}$-inch strip. A flat-tipped pen could be used to indicate the $\frac{1}{16}$-inch area that is to be cut out.

Cutting the Stained Glass

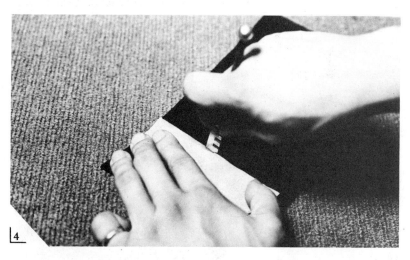

4 In preparation for cutting the stained glass, place the glass to be cut on a pile of newspapers, several layers of felt, or a flat thick piece of carpet. Dip the glass cutting wheel into a little all-purpose oil or kerosene to lubricate it. Hold the glass cutter at a right angle to the glass you are cutting. Cut on the smooth side of the glass if you are using Cathedral glass. Follow the shape of your pattern, making one cut at a time. Press firmly as you draw the wheel across the glass. You will hear a cutting (scratching) sound. Lift up as you come to the edge of the glass so you do not chip it.

5   With the ball end of the glass cutter, gently tap the reverse side of the glass along the cut. This will cause a crack in the glass. Notice the crack in the center of the cut in the photograph. Keep tapping along the cut until the crack extends completely along the line you have cut.

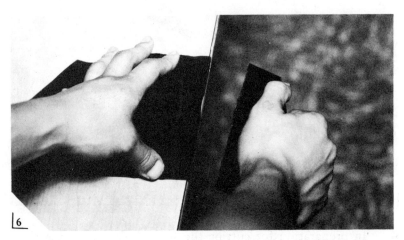

6   Place the stained glass on the edge of the table with the cut side of the glass on top. Hold the piece on the edge of the table

firmly with one hand and pull down on the extended section with the other hand. Glass can be broken in the hand, also. Remember to have the cut on top and break down on both sides of the cut, pushing the cut section up with your thumbs.

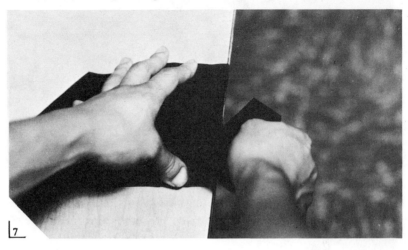

7   Brush the two pieces of glass against each other to remove the razor-sharp edge of the newly cut piece. The edges can also be filed by placing the piece on the edge of the table and doing a downward stroke with the file on the edge of the glass. Lift the file away from the glass as you come up to again do a downward filing movement.

8   Deep inner curves need to be approached slowly by gradually cutting the glass away. Make only one cut at a time. Multiple cuts will shatter the piece. Glass should be broken immediately after it has been scratched or the scratch will "heal" and close. NOTE: Circular pieces will have to be cut out gradually, if you do not have a circle cutter.

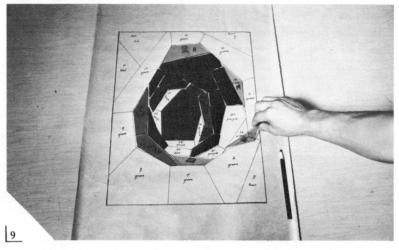

9

9 Using a grease crayon, number each cut piece of glass and place it on the corresponding number on the paper design. Save the cut paper pattern in case you need to cut a new piece due to breakage.

Enameling the Glass

10 To enamel a design on the stained glass, mix a low-fire glass decorating powder (enamel powder), usually brown, or black, with gum tragacanth or an enameling oil, using a spatula on a nonporous surface. Paint the design on the surface of the glass.

10

11

11 Paint or dust whiting or talc (calcium carbonate) on the kiln shelf so that the glass will not stick to the shelf if it melts.

Fire glass of the same color together in the enameling kiln. Different colors of glass have different melting temperatures and will absorb the enamel at a different rate of speed, so it is best to fire only one color at a time. After the glass has been placed in the cold kiln, turn the kiln on low for one hour. Then turn the kiln up to medium for one hour. After the kiln has been on medium for an hour, turn it to high and watch the enamel carefully through the peephole. When the low-fire glass powder smooths out, the piece is done. Turn the kiln off, but DO NOT REMOVE THE GLASS FROM THE KILN. Allow the glass and kiln to return to room temperature slowly; otherwise, the glass will shatter with the quick change of temperature.

Setting the Glass in the Lead Cames

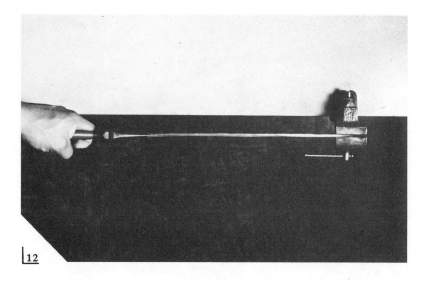

12

12 Place the lead came in a vise and pull the came with a pair of pliers to stretch and straighten it.

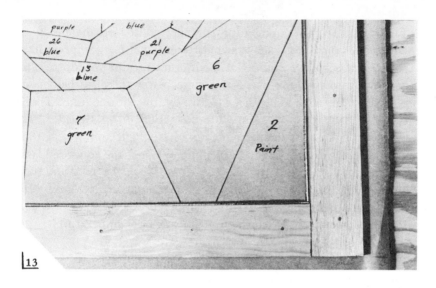

13 Place your paper design on a sheet of plywood. Nail strips of wood at right angles on one of the corners of your design. Place two U cames at right angles to each other in this corner.

14 Cut a came to the desired length by slowly rocking a knife back and forth across the top of the came until you reach the bottom. This will prevent the channel of the came from collapsing. Cut the came a little shorter than the glass piece to allow for the overlapping of other cames from other angles.

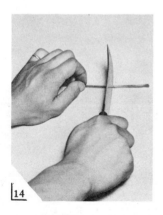

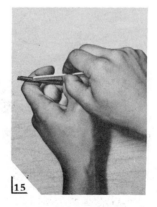

15 Open the edge of the lead came. A *lathkin* is a special tool used for this task, or you can use a tongue depressor or a popsicle stick. Avoid scratching the lead came.

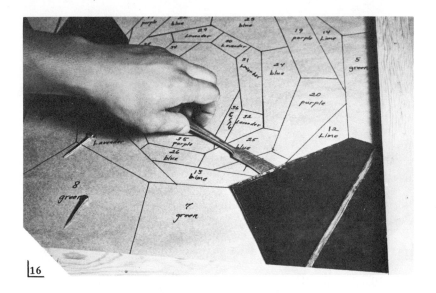

16 Slip the glass in between the top and bottom edge of the lead came. A small flat knife will help lift the glass slightly so that you can position it more easily.

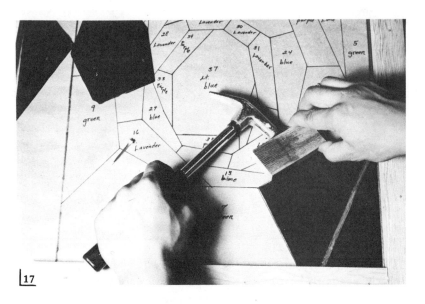

17 Place a small block of wood next to the edge of the glass and gently hammer it to force the glass against the interior edge of the channel of the lead came.

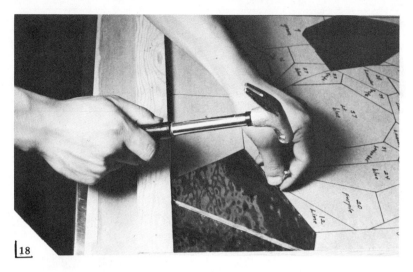

18 Place nails along the edges of the glass to hold them in place temporarily. As glass and cames are added, remove the nails and replace them along the new edges.

Tinning a Soldering Iron

19 If you are using a new soldering tip or new soldering iron, the tip needs to be *tinned* to prepare it for soldering work. To do this, dip the tip in the oleic acid and then coat the soldering iron with the solder that is to be used for the stained glass work. Wipe it off occasionally on a cloth and repeat the process until the surface of the tip is dulled in sheen.

Soldering the Cames

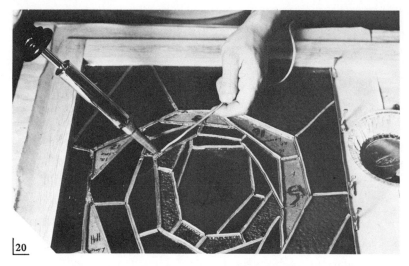

20 Using a wire brush, clean each area to be soldered; apply the oleic acid to each joint as you solder it. With a soldering iron or propane torch, melt the wire solder on each joint. Avoid touching the glass with the soldering iron; the heat from the soldering iron could crack the glass. If you should crack a piece of glass, recut the piece. Remove the nails and lead came and glass to insert the new piece of glass in the desired area. It is advisable to work from the corner with the nailed boards toward the other edges, thus, if you should break a piece of glass, it will be easier to get to and remove.

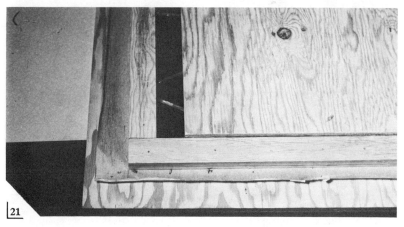

21 After one side has been soldered, remove all the nails and place a piece of plywood or masonite over the glass panel and flip it over to the other side. Solder the other side of the panel.

22

22   After the piece has been completely soldered, push the stained glass putty between the cames and the stained glass on both sides of the window. This helps to support the lead cames, which are very flexible. Use a pointed stick, such as an orange stick, to remove the excess putty on both sides of the glass panel. If too much solder has been applied, wrap a piece of wet/dry sandpaper around the small wooden block previously used and sand the solder flat. Try to avoid scratching the stained glass while you do this.

23

23   Sprinkle whiting or talc (calcium carbonate) or a cleaning and polishing powder over the surface of the panel. Using a scrub brush, remove any remaining putty. Do this on both sides of the glass panel.

24 Set the glass panel in a wide wood frame with a standing base or in a window opening.

FURTHER SUGGESTIONS

Stained glass projects may be large or small. If you are just beginning and wish to do a small project, a simulated stained glass project can be done using adhesive copper foil instead of lead cames. The adhesive foil comes in narrow strips and can be strengthened by coating it with solder after it has been applied to the edges of the stained glass. This technique would be useful in making small medallions for necklaces or Christmas tree ornaments. A fused enamel could be used to create images on medallions.

Stained glass can also be temporarily sandwiched between layers of oil clay, such as children use. The outer edge (about ¼ inch) of the stained glass is left exposed. These sandwiched pieces can be laid in a mold, bordered with oil clay, and epoxy mixed with a filler can be poured around the sandwiched pieces of stained glass. When the epoxy has cured, the oil clay can be removed and the glass will be recessed within the epoxy. A standing open wooden frame can be constructed around this stained glass piece. An example of this is shown in the author's work "Mystical Body" at the beginning of this chapter.

Another possibility for stained glass is to fuse two or more pieces together by placing the pieces in an enameling kiln. Regular enamels used in copper enameling could be used between pieces of glass. The entire inner side of one piece of stained glass can be coated with a powdered opaque enamel and a design can be created by either pulling a pointed instrument through the powdered enamel or by using a paper stencil before putting the powdered opaque enamel on the one side. If the paper stencil is used, lift the stencil off after the powdered enamel has been applied. Next, place a similar color of stained glass on top of the powdered enamel, and place the two pieces of glass in the enameling kiln to be fused together. Other possibilities would include using transparent colored enamels on the stained glass, either by themselves or incorporated with opaque enamels.

GLOSSARY

Abstract—an image of an object that has a realistic form as its basis, but has been simplified, with details omitted

Acrylic—a plastic that softens with heat (thermoplastic); comes in sheets, rods, balls, and liquid and powdered form; methyl methacrylate; a clear plastic that can be dyed with opaque or transparent dyes while in the liquid state; also a paint

Air Bubbles—pockets of air that, when trapped in clay or enamels, will expand with heat, and, in the case of clay, will cause the piece to shatter

Analogous—colors that are next to each other on the color wheel (e.g., blue-green, blue, blue-violet)

Antique Glass—stained glass, containing tiny air bubbles, that was originally a blown cylinder that has been cut in half and allowed to flatten in the heat of a kiln

Appliqué—a piece of cloth sewn to another larger piece of fabric; or the act of sewing a smaller piece of cloth to a larger piece of fabric

Basse Taille—a technique in enameling; a metal surface that has a design etched or engraved in it with a transparent colored enamel covering it

Batik—a method of preventing dye from entering fabric by covering areas with hot wax or other dye resistant liquids; fabric dyed in the above manner

Bats—(see *Plaster Bats*)

Beater—a device that holds a reed and is used to separate warp threads and beat weft threads into a horizontal position

Bernzomatic Torch—a clean-burning hand torch that uses propane gas

Beveler—a tool used for reducing the thickness of leather

Biscuit Ware—clay that has been fired once

Bisque Ware—(see *Biscuit Ware*)

Bobbin—yarn, thread, or twine looped together by hand to form a "butterfly" or wound around another form to provide a large source of yarn, thread, or twine in a small compact area; a form around which yarn, twine, or thread is wound

Came—(see *Lead Came*)

Cartoon—a simple outline drawing used in mosaics and stained glass

Cathedral Glass—colored glass that is pressed between rollers and embossed on one side with a texture while the glass is in a molten state

Champlevé—an enameling technique; a metal surface containing recessed areas filled with opaque colored enamels

Cloisonné—an enameling technique; a metal surface of colored enamel separated by narrow metal wires (cloisons)

Cloisons—strips of flat gold, silver, or copper wire that are used to create a design on a metal surface in cloisonné enameling

Closed Design—an object or image that is self-contained or bears a close resemblance to the form from which it came

Coil Method—creating long, snake-like rolls of clay that are then joined together to form a ceramic piece

Cold Water Dyes—dyes that can be applied cold to a fabric

Complementary—colors that are directly opposite each other on the color wheel (e.g., green and red)

Cones—(see *Pyrometric Cones*)

Crackle Effect—a cracked design effect in batik achieved by allowing dye to run into the areas of wax that have been cracked

Dalles—(see *Slab Glass*)

Design—may be a motif or a repeated motif

Discharge Dyeing—removing dye from a fabric by bleaching or using a color remover

Earthenware—a coarse, low-fire clay body that is porous after firing

Embroidery—decorative stitches of thread or yarn on the surface of a fabric; the act of stitching thread or yarn to a fabric

Enamel—transparent or opaque powdered or ground glass which, when melted in a kiln between 1350°F. and 1550°F., will form a glass surface on metal or another piece of glass

Enameling Fork—a two-pronged, long handled tool used for placing wire screens holding enamel pieces into the kiln

Engobe—a colored clay body (slip) used in decorating greenware—see *Sgraffito*

Epoxy Resin—a thermosetting resin that has flexibility under heat and stress to allow for different expansion and contraction coefficients of the materials it binds together; it is usually a transparent straw color and can be colored with opaque and transparent dyes while in the liquid state

Ethylene Dichloride—a solvent used for cementing acrylic pieces together

Faceted Glass—(see *Slab Glass*)

Fetish—a primitive object used as a protection for a person or place or having power (*mana*) of its own

Fettling Knife—a long, flat, triangular bladed knife used in ceramic work to cut and trim clay pieces

Fire Scale—flaky material or discoloration resulting from the oxidation of metal by fire and heat

Flash—extra material from a casting that is found around the edge of the casting or along the edges where two pieces of a mold join together

Flashed Glass—a type of stained glass that has color adhered to the surfaces of the glass that can be clear or a lighter color than the color flashed on the surfaces

Free Form—usually a curved form that can be open or closed

Frisket—a simple paper or rubber design that is used to cover areas where a glaze or enamel or other colored material is not desired; this is lifted off prior to the firing or glaze firing process

Geometric—angular and rounded forms and shapes that can be mathematically calculated or created with measuring instruments such as a ruler, compass, etc.

Glaze—powdered chemicals, metallic oxides, and a gum solution mixed with water that will produce a transparent or opaque, a matte or shiny surface on a ceramic piece

Greenware—clay that is dry but has not been fired

Grisaille—an enameling technique; an enameled white image of varying thickness and transparency on the black or dark enameled background of a metal surface that results in an image similar to those found on Wedgewood ceramic pieces

Grog—clay that has been fired once and is ground into sand-like particles; these particles are then placed in fresh clay to create *grogged clay*

Grout—a fine cement powder that is mixed with water and used for filling in the crevices between tiles in mosaic pieces

Harness—a device containing heddles, which hold some warp threads—creates a *shed*, when lifted

Heddles—found within the open frame of a harness, these are vertical strips with a hole in the center of each through which one warp thread passes

Kapok—a soft cotton used for stuffing

Kiln Furniture—stilts, shelves, racks, etc. for a kiln

Kiln Wash—a liquid that is applied to kiln shelves for enameling and ceramic glazing to protect the shelves from enamel and glaze droppings

Lacing—narrow strips of leather from $3/32$-inch to $3/16$-inch wide that are used for joining pieces of leather together; process of joining leather pieces together with narrow strips of leather

Lead Came—a strip of lead with a channel on one or both sides for holding stained glass pieces in place

Limoges—an enameling technique; a colorful painted enamel image on a metal surface; enameling technique that originated in Limoges, France

Loom—a device for holding warp threads while weaving weft thread through them

Macramé—yarn, twine, or thread knotted with the hands

Mallet—a hammer-like instrument with a cylindrical head made of wood or rawhide

Mastic—a water-resistant adhesive used for setting tiles in floors and walls; it is flammable and fast drying

Mica—a sheet-like mineral that can withstand high temperatures and is used as a backing in *plique-a-jour* enameling to hold the powdered enamel in place during the firing process, but is peeled off the enamel piece after the firing has been completed

Monochromatic—use of one color and its tints and shades (e.g., orange, peach, rust)

Mordant—a chemical, usually an acid, that is used to "lock in" the dye on a fabric; also used to etch metal

Mortar—a concrete or cement mixture used in mosaic work

Mortar and Pestle—a bowl and a rod that is bulbous on one end that is used for grinding and mixing glazes to a fine consistency

Mosaic—a surface consisting of small pieces of material, such as glass, tiles, wood, or plastics

Motif—a single design that can be repeated

Nichrome Wire—a high temperature wire that will not acquire fire scale during firing; used for holding beads or may be inserted into soft fire brick to create holders for objects during the firing process

Nonobjective—having no object for its basis; without reference to reality or natural objects

Open Design—an image or object that has extensions emanating from its axial line or the center of the form, or an object or image containing many holes or openings

Organic—following natural growth patterns or shapes and forms of living things

Organic Material—matter of plant or animal origins

Pattern—repeated motif

Pestle—(see *Mortar and Pestle*)

Pinch Pot—a ceramic pot created by pinching the clay with the fingers and hands

Plain Weave—a simple over-and-under weaving of weft threads through the warp threads

Plaiting—braiding

Plaster Bats—flat forms that have been cast of plaster of Paris; used in clay work to absorb moisture from the clay

Plique-a-jour—an enameling technique; a metal piece containing small openings cut through the metal that are filled with transparent colored enamels; when it is held up to the light, it is like a miniature stained glass window

Polyester Resin—a thermosetting liquid plastic that is clear but can be colored with opaque or transparent dyes; can be used as an adhesive, a binder, a matrix, and for waterproofing in mosaic work

Propane Torch—(see *Bernzomatic Torch*)

Pyrometric Cones—long, triangular clay pieces that melt at different temperatures; used to indicate the interior temperature of a ceramic kiln during the firing process

Reed—vertical slats set in the beater that separate warp threads and beat the weft threads straight

Registration—making certain that two or more colors will align correctly through the use of key marks on the edges of each of the colored images

Sgraffito—a technique used in ceramics and enameling; in ceramics a colored engobe is placed on greenware and then scratched through to reveal the original clay body; in enameling a second color is laid over another color that has been fired and a pointed instrument is used to scratch the second layer off in areas or lines to reveal the first color

Shed—the opening created in the warp when some of the warp threads are lifted by a set of heddles in a harness

Shuttle—a device that carries the twine, yarn, or thread used as the filling, weft, or woof across the warp threads of the loom

Silk Screen—an open box across which is stretched a loosely woven fabric through which ink is forced onto a surface

Skiver (Skife)—a tool with a razor blade that is used for removing excess leather in areas or thinning the ends of lacing

Slab Glass—thick pieces of glass (½- to 2- or more inches thick) that are chipped by a special hammer, which creates facets along the edge of the glass, giving it the name *faceted glass*; due to the thickness of the glass it is usually set in concrete or epoxy rather than in lead cames

Slab Method—a ceramic technique in which clay is rolled out flat between two slats of wood of equal thickness to create a slab, which is then joined to similar slabs to create a ceramic piece

Slip—clay to which water has been added until it has the consistency of thick cream; used for casting in molds or joining clay pieces together

Spacer—a tool that will make equidistant marks on a surface

Spatula—a broad, flat, knife-like implement used for lifting small objects, stirring, or laying in color areas

Squeegee—a strip of wood that has a strip of rubber set in one of its edges; used in the silk screening process to force ink through the screen

Stained Glass—colored glass that consists of metallic oxides, silica, iron, limestone, borax, and soda ash which, when melted together, forms colored glass—see *Antique Glass, Flashed Glass, Cathedral Glass*, and *Slab Glass*

Stencil—an image that prevents color from reaching a certain area—see *Frisket*

Stitchery—the use of embroidery and appliqué to create a surface of textural variety or integration

Stoneware—a fine-grained, high-fire clay body that is nonporous after firing

Symmetrical—when a design or object is halved, both sides are mirror images of each other

Tesserae—small pieces (originally marble) used in making a mosaic

Texture—surface quality of an object

Tie Dye—a technique of binding fabric with strips of cloth, twine, or thread to prevent dye from entering the area of the fabric that is tied

Tjanting Tool—a rod at the end of which is a small cup with a spout that holds hot wax that is used in the batik process

Tooling—embossing leather with a design that has raised and lowered sections

Triadic—three colors equidistant from each other on the color wheel (e.g., red, yellow, blue)

Turnbuckle—a metal piece containing screws on both ends; when the center metal piece is revolved, the screws on both ends are pulled toward the center or are released outward, either tightening the wires it has been attached to or loosening them

Undercuts—extensions or indentations in a three-dimensional form that prevent its easy removal from a mold

Warp—vertical threads, yarn, or twine across which the weft or filling is woven

Warping Board—a device or a board with pegs, around which long lengths of warp can be measured off in a small space

Weaving—interlacing threads at right angles to each other to create a textile

Wedging—throwing clay with force on a flat surface to remove the air bubbles in the clay; clay can be wedged by kneading it

Weft—horizontal threads, yarn, or twine woven across the warp threads; sometimes referred to as the *filling* or *woof*

Whiting—calcium carbonate that is dusted or painted on enameling kiln shelves or ceramic molds to protect them while melting glass

Woof—(see *Weft*)

appendix b

ADDRESSES OF SUPPLIERS

Code	Addresses	Chapters	Comments
AAC	American Art Clay Company, Inc. 4717 West Sixteenth Street Indianapolis, Indiana 46222	Acrylic Casting, Enameling, Stained Glass, Ceramics	Also called AMACO Ceramic supply house
ACC	Arts & Crafts Colony 4132 N. Tamiami Trail Sarasota, Florida 33580	Enameling, Ceramics, Textile Silk Screening	Ceramic supply house
AH	American Handicrafts 3157 Wilshire Boulevard Los Angeles, California 90005	Mosaics, Stained Glass, Acrylic Casting, Enameling	Located in all states except Hawaii and Alaska
ATS	Allcraft Tool and Supply Company Hicksville, New York 11801	Tie Dye, Acrylic Casting, Enameling, Mosaics, Stained Glass	Other locations: 204 North Harbor Blvd., Fullerton, California 92632
BAC	Bergen Arts & Crafts Box 381 Marblehead, Massachusetts 01945	Moasics, Stained Glass, Batik, Tie Dye, Enameling, Acrylic Casting, Ceramics	Ceramic supply house
BG	Brodhead-Garret Company 4560 East 71st Street Cleveland, Ohio 44105	Acrylic Casting, Tie Dye, Stained Glass, Weaving, Leathercraft, Enameling, Batik, Ceramics	Ceramic supply house
BGC	Blenko Glass Company Milton, West Virginia 25541	Stained Glass	
BI	Bartlettyarns, Inc. Harmony, Maine 04942	Weaving	
BLC	Berman Leather Company 145-147 South Street Boston, Massachusetts 02111	Leathercraft	
CCI	The Craftool Company Inc. 1421 W. 240th Street Harbor City, California 90810	Batik, Acrylic Casting, Enameling, Ceramics	Ceramic supply house

Code	Supplier	Category	Notes
CH	Custom Handweavers c/o Enid Wood Allied Arts Guild Arbor Road and Creek Drive Menlo Park, California 94025	Weaving, Macramé, Stitchery	Supply "goody Bags" for small weaving and stitchery projects
CHL	Ceramics Hawaii Ltd. 629 C Cooke Street Honolulu, Hawaii 96813	Enameling, Ceramics	Ceramic supply house
CRH	C.R. Hill Company 2734 W. 11 Mile Road Berkley, Michigan 48072	Enameling	
CWC	Carpenter & Wood Company, Inc. 15 Cedar Street Providence, Rhode Island 02903	Enameling	
CY	Contessa Yarns P.O. Box 37 Lebanon, Connecticut 06249	Weaving	
DCP	Duncan Ceramic Products Inc. P.O. Box 7827 Fresno, California 93727	Ceramics	Ceramic supply house Located in all United States of America, Canada, Puerto Rico, and many foreign countries
DCS	Denwar Craft Studio 236 East 16th Street Costa Mesa, California 92627	Mosaics	Supply hand made ceramic tiles
DI	Dap, Inc. 5300 Huberville Road Dayton, Ohio 45431	Stained Glass	Dap "33 Gray" Glazing Compound
DTC	Dharma Trading Company P.O. Box 1288 Berkeley, California 94701	Tie Dye, Batik	

Code	Addresses	Chapters	Comments
EH	Economy Handicrafts 47-11 Francis Lewis Boulevard Flushing, New York 11361	Textile Silk Screening, Mosaics, Batik, Tie Dye, Stained Glass, Enameling, Leathercraft, Acrylic Casting, Ceramics	Ceramic supply house Other locations: 50-21 69th Street Woodside, New York 11377
ESC	Electrical Specialty Company (A General Electric Distributor) 213 E. Harris Avenue South San Francisco, California 94080	Acrylic Casting	General Electric's RTV-630 A & B Silicone mold material
F	FAB DEC P.O. Box 201 Ingram, Texas 78025	Tie Dye, Batik	
GG	Gems Galore (Retail) W.H. Haney Company (Industrial and Wholesale) 240 Castro Street Mountain View, California 94040	Acrylic Casting, Leathercraft	
HBM	Handy Button Machine Co. of N.Y., Inc. 50-05 47th Avenue Woodside, New York 11377	Leathercraft	
JDW	Jack D. Wolfe Co., Inc. 724-734 Meeker Aenue Brooklyn, New York 11222	Enameling, Ceramics, Stained Glass	Ceramic supply house
JLH	J.L. Hammett Company Hammett Place Braintree, Massachusetts 02184	Tie Dye, Batik, Weaving, Enameling, Acrylic Casting, Ceramics	Ceramic supply house Other locations: Vauxhall Road Union, N.J. 07083 165 Water Street Lyons, N.Y. 14489 Box 4125 Lynchburg, Va. 24502

KSS	Kilns Supply & Service Corp. 38 Bulkley Avenue P.O. Box 1071 Port Chester, New York 10573	Ceramics	Boston store: 48 Canal Street Boston, Mass. 02114 Ceramic supply house The home of "NORMAN KILNS"
LMC	Lily Mills Company Hand Weaving Department Shelby, North Carolina 28150	Weaving	Also supply macramé cords, rug canvas, and mono canvas
MAA	Macomber AD-A-HARNESS LOOMS® 566-570 Lincoln Avenue Saugus, Massachusetts 01906	Weaving	Ceramic supply house
MAC	Macmillan Arts & Crafts, Inc. 9520 Baltimore Avenue College Park, Maryland 20740	Textile Silk Screening, Stained Glass, Batik, Leathercraft, Tie Dye, Acrylic Casting, Ceramics, Enameling, Mosaics	
MSC	M. Siegel Company Inc. 186 South Street Boston, Massachusetts 02111	Leathercraft	Also supply brass buckles and rings, pewter buckles, craft cement, nylon thread
NDC	Naz-Dar Company 1087 N. North Branch Street Chicago, Illinois 60622	Textile Silk Screening	
NLC	Norwood Loom Company Box 272 Baldwin, Michigan 49304	Weaving	They build looms.
NPS	Newton Potters Supply Inc. P.O. Box 724 724 Main Street Waltham, Massachusetts 02154	Ceramics	Ceramic supply house

Code	Addresses	Chapters	Comments
NS	Nervo Studios 2027 7th Street Berkeley, California 94710	Stained Glass	Ceramic supply house
SAC	Sax Arts and Crafts P.O. Box 2002 Milwaukee, Wisconsin 53201	Enameling, Mosaics, Acrylic Casting, Batik, Tie Dye, Weaving, Leathercraft, Ceramics, Textile Silk Screening	
SC	Sieg Camlott Artistic Glass 315 East 2100 South Salt Lake City, Utah 84115	Stained Glass	Also supplies: Leading hammers, small grozing pliers, lead stretcher (lead-vise)
SCC	Stewart Clay Company, Inc. 133 Mulberry Street New York, New York 10013	Mosaics, Enameling, Ceramics	Ceramic supply house
SCP	Standard Ceramic Supply Company P.O. Box 4435 Pittsburgh, Pennsylvania 15205	Ceramics	Ceramic supply house
SGC	The Stained Glass Club P.O. Box 244 Norwood, New Jersey 07648	Stained Glass	
SI	Swest Incorporated 10803 Composite Drive P.O. Box 2010 Dallas, Texas 75221	Acrylic Casting, Enameling	Formerly Southwest Smelting & Refining Company, Inc. Other locations: 118 Broadway P.O. Box 1298 San Antonio, Texas 78206 1725 Victory Blvd. Los Angeles (Glendale), California 91201

SOC	Stewart's of California, Inc. 16055 Heron Avenue La Mirada, California 90638	Ceramics	Ceramic supply house
SPS	Screen Process Supplies Mfg. Co. 1199 East 12th Street Oakland, California 94606	Textile Silk Screening	Manufacturer of screen printing inks, equipment, and supplies; sell through dealers also.
TAC	Triarco Arts & Crafts (Formerly: J.C. Larson Co.) 7330 North Clark Street Chicago, Illinois 60626	Batik, Mosaics, Tie Dye, Textile Silk Screening, Stained Glass, Ceramics, Leathercraft, Enameling, Acrylic Casting	Ceramic supply house Other locations: 1000 Troy Court Troy, Michigan 48084 3516 Beltline Blvd. St. Louis Park, Minn. 55416 4146 Library Road Pittsburgh, Pa. 15244 1839 West Broad St. Richmond, Va. 23220 136 Preston Valley Shopping Center Dallas, Texas 75230 5737 38th Ave. North St. Petersburg, Florida 33510
TCT	Thomas C. Thompson Company 1539 Deerfield Road P.O. Box 127 Highland Park, Illinois 60035	Stained Glass, Enameling, Acrylic Casting	
TLC	Tandy Leather Company 1001 Foch Street Fort Worth, Texas 76107	Leathercraft	Outlets in all states except Hawaii and Alaska.

Code	Addresses	Chapters	Comments
TYD	The Yarn Depot 545 Sutter Street San Francisco, California 94102	Weaving, Stitchery	
WCC	W. Cushing & Co. Kennebunkport, Maine 04046	Batik, Tie Dye	Cushing "Perfection" Dyes are hot water dyes but when cooled can be used for batik dyeing.
WCS	Western Ceramics Supply Company 1601 Howard Street San Francisco, California 94103	Ceramics, Stained Glass, Enameling, Acrylic Casting	Ceramic supply house
WDG	Whittemore-Durgin Glass Company Box 2065 EQ Hanover, Massachusetts 02339	Stained Glass	

appendix c

BIBLIOGRAPHY

DESIGNING

Guyler, Vivian Varney. *Design in Nature*. Worchester, Mass.: Art Resources Publications, a Division of Davis Publications, Inc., 1970.

Provides design sources found in nature that could be used for craft projects.

Maurello, S. Ralph, ed. *Introduction to the Visual Arts*. New York: Tudor Publishing Company, 1968.

Presents and explores basic design fundamentals. An excellent source for design development for the beginning craftsman.

Wolberg, Lewis R., M.D. *Micro-Art: Art Images in a Hidden World*. New York: Harry N. Abrams, Inc.

An inspirational book of microphotographs that could easily be used as a creative source for weaving, macramé, stitchery, as well as other crafts.

IDEA BOOKS

Hughes, Graham, *Modern Jewelry: An International Survey 1890-1963*. New York: Crown Publishers, Inc., 1963.

An international presentation of the work of jewelers in metal throughout the world. A source of inspiration for the craftsman.

Morton, Philip. *Contemporary Jewelry: A Studio Handbook.* San Francisco: Holt, Rinehart and Winston, Inc., 1969.

An excellent technical and creative book offering a short historical survey in jewelry as well as examples of contemporary jewelry. Provides in-depth information on designing and techniques for casting, soldering, electroforming, setting stones and setting up shop in jewelry work. Sources of supplies are listed, as well as other technical data.

Slivka, Rose, ed. *The Crafts of the Modern World*. New York: Horizon Press, 1968.

A visual and verbal exploration of the variety of crafts that are found throughout the world. A graphic presentation of the variety of approaches to materials by people of different countries.

Sommer, Elyse. *Contemporary Costume Jewelry: A Multimedia Approach.* New York: Crown Publishers, Inc., 1974.

An exploration of jewelry making in a variety of materials such as metal, wood, glass, plastics, clay, fabrics, fiber, leather.

Van Dommelen, David B. *Decorative Wall Hangings: Art With Fabric.* New York: Funk & Wagnalls Company, Inc., 1962.

Creatively presents a variety of media used for wall hangings: batik, tie dye, stitchery, weaving, stenciling, hooking, collage, and so on. A list of suppliers is given as well as a brief historical survey of wall hangings and stitchery work.

Willcox, Donald J. *Body Jewelry: International Perspectives.* Chicago: Henry Regnery Company, 1973.

A beautifully illustrated book featuring the work of jewelry craftsmen from around the world. A book designed to open the mind to new concepts in jewelry design.

TIE DYE

Maile, Anne. *Tie and Dye as a Present-Day Craft.* New York: Ballantine Books, 1971.

An excellent book with many suggestions as to how to tie fabric in various ways to achieve different results.

BATIK

The "Writing" of Batik. Woodridge, N.J.: Craftools, Inc., 1968.

Presents a clearly explained method for doing batik along with a brief introduction to the possible origins of batik and its use in Java.

Martin, Beryl. *Batik for Beginners.* New York: Charles Scribner's Sons, 1971.

Described the symbolic use of batik designs on fabric in Java; discusses the tools used for batik work; and gives a clear explanation of how the work is done. Lavishly illustrated with color and black and white photos.

Stein, Vivian. *Batik as a Hobby*. New York: Sterling Publishing Company, Inc., 1969.

Gives directions and projects for batik work. A brief historical survey is also presented.

STITCHERY

One Hundred Embroidery Stitches: Book No. 150. New York: Coats and Clark's.

Easy to follow drawn diagrams show embroidery stitches, drawn work, and needlepoint.

Beitler, Ethel Jane. *Create With Yarn*. Scranton, Pa.: International Textbook Company, 1964.

Shows a variety of embroidery stitches as well as creative stitchery pieces and knotted and hooked rugs and tapestry weaving.

Butler, Anne. *Embroidery Stitches: An Illustrated Guide*. New York: Frederick A. Praeger, 1968.

A very inspirational book containing drawings and photographs of embroidery stitches and showing their use in final projects.

Christie, Mrs. Archibald. *Samplers and Stitches: A Handbook of the Embroiderer's Art*. London: B. T. Batsford, Limited, 1920.

A variety of embroidery stitches are presented and very clearly diagramed. Finished samplers are shown using the stitches diagramed. A marvelous handbook showing the possibilities of thread on fabric.

Douglass, Winsome. *Discovering Embroidery*. London: Mills & Boon Limited, 1955.

Shows drawings of embroidery stitches and possible projects to be done utilizing embroidery work, also includes drawn work, quilting, smocking, and various edgings.

Gonsalves, Alyson Smith, and Lynne R. Morrall, eds. *Stitchery: Embroidery, Applique, Crewel*. Menlo Park, Calif.: Lane Publishing Company, 1974.

Types of fabric for stitchery and types of thread and yarns are photographically presented along with detailed drawings of a variety of embroidery and sewing machine stitches. Gives creative examples and projects with patterns.

Howard, Constance. *Inspiration for Embroidery*. Newton Centre, Mass.: Charles T. Branford Company, 1967.

A book showing design development for stitchery. Many excellent ideas are presented here that are very professional in their applications. Suggestions for clothing decorations are given showing a relationship of design to the form on which it is placed. A list of suppliers is provided.

Jacopetti, Alexandra. *Native Funk & Flash: An Emerging Folk Art*. San Francisco: Scrimshaw Press, 1974.

This book is in full color! Very creative projects are shown—one took two years to embroider. Mosaics, jewelry, woodwork, batik, bread dough creations, and decorative building paintings are also included with beautiful examples of stitchery work.

Karasz, Mariska. *A New Art of Embroidery: Adventures in Stitches, and More Adventures—Fewer Stitches* 2d ed. New York: Funk & Wagnalls Company, 1949.

A variety of stitches are shown along with a creative use of embroidery in stitchery work. Various types of yarns are identified.

Krevitsky, Nik. *Stitchery: Art and Craft*. New York: Reinhold Publishing Corporation, 1966.

A marvelously creative book on stitchery showing pictorially how natural designs can be developed into a craft form. A creative exploration of yarn, thread, and twine incorporated with cloth.

Laury, Jean Ray. *Applique Stitchery*. New York: Reinhold Publishing Corporation, 1966.

An excellent presentation on where to look for ideas as well as how to apply the art elements to a stitchery piece. Well illustrated with color and black and white photographs and drawings. Shows embroidery stitches and details on finishing projects.

Laury, Jean Ray and Joyce Aiken. *Creating Body Coverings*. New York: Van Nostrand Reinhold Company, 1973.

This inspirational book shows the creative possibilities of stitchery. Besides stitchery, tie-dye, crocheting, batik, silk screening, and even tattooing (!) are covered in this book.

Scrase, Pat. *Let's Start Designing*. New York: Reinhold Publishing Corporation, 1966.

> Gives creative ideas to pursue in designing or decorating objects. Presents adaptation of designs for stitchery work as well as a section devoted to embroidery stitches.

Seyd, Mary. *Designing With String*. New York: Watson-Guptill Publications, 1967.

> An excellent book exploring the possibilities of string, yarn, and twine as a creative medium. Photographs show the creative possibilities of the medium. Sources of supplies are also given.

TEXTILE SILK SCREENING

Inko Silk Screen Printing: Materials & Techniques. Oakland, Calif.: Screen Process Supplies Manufacturing Company, 1971.

> A combination catalog and technique manual covering all aspects of screening, including photo screening. A list of design and screen process printing books are given in an annotated bibliography.

MACRAMÉ

Alfers, Betty. *Macramé*. New York: Grosset & Dunlap, 1971.

> Explains some of the more basic knots used in macramé work.

Harvey, Virginia I. *Color and Design in Macramé*. New York: Van Nostrand Reinhold Company, 1967.

> This book shows some very creative projects using basic macramé knots. The possibilities of the use of color in macramé work are shown in some very inventive projects.

Hensel, John. *The Book of Ornamental Knots*. New York: Charles Scribner's Sons, 1973.

> This book contains very clearly photographed steps showing how to make various ornamental knots. An excellent "follow-up" book for one who knows macramé and would enjoy doing something more challenging. Supply sources are also listed.

Pesch, Imelda Manalo. Macramé: Creative Knotting. New York: Sterling Publishing Company, Inc., 1970.

Basic knots as well as ideas for projects in macramé are given.

Phillips, Mary Walker. *Step-By-Step Macramé*. New York: Golden Press, 1970.

Presents basic macramé knots and directions for specific projects as well as creative examples of the use of macramé. A list of suppliers is provided as well as schools and workshops offering macramé.

Short, Eirian. *Introducing Macramé*. New York: Watson-Guptill Publications, 1970.

Historical background of macramé is presented along with a variety of knots and very creative and imaginative projects. A list of suppliers in Great Britain is also given.

WEAVING

Black, Mary E. *Weaving for Beginners*. Ottawa, Canada: The Queen's Printer, 1966.

A very useful handbook for a person beginning on a floor loom. It covers how to thread the loom to how to complete the weaving and remove it from the loom. Contains a glossary of terms and lists sources of suppliers in various Canadian provinces.

Chetwynd, Hilary. *Simple Weaving*. New York: Watson-Guptill Publications, 1969.

A very clear visual and verbal explanation of weaving terms and techniques, including a clear presentation of pattern drafting for weaving. Explains how to calculate the amount of yarn needed. Gives a list of suppliers for both England and the United States.

Francisco, Irene. *Opening A Door to Two Harness Techniques*. Shelby, N.C.: Lily Mills Company, 1960.

Shows lace and inlay techniques that a beginner can use on a two-harness table loom. Inlay work is also explained.

Rainey, Sarita R. *Weaving Without a Loom*. Worchester, Mass.: Davis Publications, Inc., 1966.

A very creative exploration into ways of weaving without a loom. Rug hooking and knotting are also shown. Contains a list of suppliers and a glossary.

Wilson, Jean. *Weaving Is for Anyone*. New York: Von Nostrand Reinhold Company, 1967.

Provides a glossary of terms at the beginning of the book. Suggests many ideas on the construction of simple looms. Gives suggestions as to what to weave and various weaving and knotting techniques on the looms.

Znamierowski, Nell. *Step-by-Step Weaving: A Complete Introduction to the Craft of Weaving*. New York: Golden Press, 1967.

An excellent book on weaving—covers types of looms dyeing yarns, warping, preparing the filling, weaving on a four-harness loom and a frame loom, and various projects on these two types of looms. Provides a glossary and a list of suppliers.

PLASTICS

Newman, Thelma R. *Plastics as An Art Form*. Philadelphia, Pa.: Chilton Books, 1964.

A technically orientated book showing the possibilities of plastics as an art form. Includes a glossary and trade names and manufacturers.

ENAMELING

Metal Enameling. Booklet No. 7, rev. ed. Indianapolis, Ind.: American Art Clay Company, Inc., 1970.

A combination "how to" and supply catalog. Clearly presents the various enameling techniques and explains defects in enameling and how to overcome them.

Bates, Kenneth F. *Enameling: Principles and Practice*. Cleveland: The World Publishing Company, 1951.

Presents a history of enameling. Also covers enameling materials and techniques. Well illustrated with many examples of each technique.

Choate, Sharr and Bonnie Cecil De May. *Creative Gold- and Silversmithing: Jewelry, Decorative Metalcraft*. New York: Crown Publishers, 1970.

Covers enameling techniques as well as electroplating, spinning, forging, scroll work, decorating techniques and inlay work. Many examples of hooking, clasps, pendant holders, and linkages, as well as ideas on stone mountings are given.

Harper, William. *Step-by-Step Enameling: A Complete Introduction to the Craft of Enameling*. New York: Golden Press, 1973.

Presents a visual and historical background as well as a very clear definition of enameling techniques, materials, and methods. A very colorful and inspirational book. An excellent book for an explorer in enameling techniques.

Newble, Brian. *Practical Enameling and Jewelry Work*. New York: The Viking Press (A Studio Book), 1967.

A clearly written book on enameling—covers the techniques of cloisonné, champlevé, basse taille, dusting, and a mosaic application of enamels. Discusses how to charge for one's work and gives a list of suppliers and a glossary.

von Neumann, Robert. *The Design and Creation of Jewelry*. Philadelphia: Chilton Books, 1961.

Covers basic metal working techniques. Discusses enameling and inlay work as well as creative ideas for decorating metal surfaces. An excellent section on "Stimulants for the Mind's Eye" provides ideas for further jewelry work. Provides a list of suppliers.

CERAMICS

Hofsted, Jolyon. *Step by Step Ceramics: A Complete Introduction to the Craft of Ceramics*. New York: Golden Press, 1967.

Explores decorating techniques and various methods of constructing clay objects. Contains a glossary and sources of supplies. A very useful book for the beginning ceramicist.

Hogan, Elizabeth, ed. *Ceramics: Techniques & Projects*. Menlo Park, Calif : Lane Books, 1973.

Covers techniques for hand building, raku ware, and working on a potter's wheel as well as firing techniques and includes some ideas on decoration. It also contains a glossary.

Long, Lois Culver. *Ceramic Decoration*. Indianapolis, Ind.: The American Art Clay Company, Inc., 1958.

Presents a variety of decorating techniques as well as information on ceramic mosaics and glass color firing. Contains a glossary and a list of firing defects and remedies.

Sanders, Herbert H. *How to Make Pottery and Ceramic Sculpture*, 2d ed. Menlo Park, Calif.: Lane Books, 1953.

A technical book clarifying how to do hand sculpture, wheel throwing, cast forms and how to fire a kiln and build a potter's wheel. It also gives ideas on decorating ceramics and sources of supplies and formulas for slips and glazes.

MOSAICS

Aller, Doris and Diane. *Mosaics*. Menlo Park, Calif.: Lane Books, 1959.

A variety of mterials for mosaic use are presented along with design suggestions and a variety of projects.

Lewis, Beatrice and Leslie McGuire. *Making Mosaics*. New York: Drake Publishers Inc., 1973.

Presents a brief history of mosaics along with suggestions on designing in the medium. A variety of projects are shown. A glossary and a list of suppliers are also provided.

Stribling, Mary Lou. *Mosaic Techniques: New Aspects of Fragmented Design*. New York: Crown Publishers, Inc., 1966.

A marvelously creative book that explores the use of a variety of materials for making mosaics. Discusses a multitude of uses for mosaics from jewelry to sculpture. A glossary and a list of suppliers are provided.

Young, Joseph L. *Mosaics: Principles and Practice*. New York: Reinhold Publishing Corp., 1963.

Gives very detailed pictures and directions for mosaic work. A wide variety of mosaic pieces are shown and a brief history of mosaics is given.

LEATHERCRAFT

Cherry, Raymond. *General Leathercraft*, 4th ed. Bloomington, Ill.: McKnight & McKnight Publishing Company, 1955.

An excellent introduction to leathercraft covering the techniques of tooling, carving, modeling, lacing, and sewing leather in step-by-step photographs. Also includes how to finish and care for leather. Tools are individually photographed for easy identification. Many patterns for individual projects are given at the end of the book.

Newman, Thelma R. *Leather As Art and Craft: Traditional Methods and Modern Designs*. New York: Crown Publishers, Inc., 1973.

A technical source of information on the history of the uses of leather and various types of leather, techniques of joining, decorating, and finishing. Lavishly illustrated with historical and contemporary examples of leathercraft. A glossary and source of supplies are provided.

STAINED GLASS

The Story of Stained Glass, 5th ed. Stained Glass Association of America, January, 1963.

A historical presentation of stained glass. Gives a brief description of how a leaded stained glass window is created, and how a faceted glass window is made. A glossary is provided.

Isenberg, Anita and Seymour. *How to Work in Stained Glass*. Philadelphia: Chilton Book Company, 1972.

Besides showing how to create a stained glass window, other smaller projects are suggested. Describes the copper foil method for small projects. How to repair stained glass windows is also covered.

Lips, Claude. *Art and Stained Glass*. Garden City, N.Y.: Doubleday & Company, Inc., 1973.

An excellent and thorough book written by a stained glass craftsman explaining the techniques involved in working with stained glass. Well diagramed and photographed. A glossary and a list of suppliers are given.

Metcalf, Robert and Gertrude. *Making Stained Glass: A Handbook for the Amateur and the Professional.* New York: McGraw-Hill Book Company, 1972.

A complete book covering the history and techniques of stained glass. An excellent presentation of the painting techniques used in stained glass.

Mollica, Peter. Fogel, Norm, ed. *Stained Glass Primer.* Berkeley, Calif.: Mollica Stained Glass Press, 1971.

A beginner's handbook showing through detailed photographs the different types of stained glass and each step of making a stained glass window. Contains a glossary and a bibliography.

Rothenberg, Polly. *Creative Stained Glass: Techniques for Unfired and Fired Projects.* New York: Crown Publishers, Inc., 1973.

A thorough explanation of making a leaded stained glass panel, showing everything from the cutting of the glass to the soldering of the leads and the glazing of the panel. Painting and firing of glass are included. The use of copper foil is explained as is the use of faceted glass in projects. Suppliers are listed.

Grogged clay, 166
Grout, 253

H

Half-step-dropped motif, 7-8
Harness, 103, 106, 254
Heddles, 103, 106, 254
Horizontal double half hitch, 91-93,
    97-98

K

Kapok, 52-53, 64, 254
Kiln furniture, 168-69, 254
Kilns, 168-70
Kiln wash, 254

L

Lacing, 213-14, 216-20, 227, 254
Lark's head knot, 89, 96-97
Lathkin, 236-37, 244
Lead cames, 235-36, 243-46, 254
Leathercraft, 209-29
    lacing, 213-14, 216-20, 227, 254
        double cordovan stitch, 213,
            218-20
        single cordovan stitch, 213,
            217-18
        whipstitch, 213-14, 216
    procedure, 221-29
    suppliers, 215
    supplies, 214-15
    tooling, 222-23, 256
    types of leather, 211-12
Light, 15-16
Limoges, 254
Looms, 105-26, 254

M

Macramé, 83-99, 254
    amount of cord needed, 86-87,
        96-97
    bobbins, 88

Macramé (continued)
    knots, 88-96
        cavandoli stitch, 85, 93-96
        diagonal double half hitch, 93
        double half hitch, 91-93
        horizontal double half hitch,
            91-93, 97, 98
        lark's head, 89, 96-97
        overhand knot, 88-89
        square knot, 89-91
        vertical double half hitch, 93,
            95, 97
    planning designs, 96-97
    suppliers, 87
    supplies, 86-87
    symbols for knots, 97
    type of cord, 86
Mallet, 214-15, 254
Mastic, 254
Mica, 254
Mola, 48
Monochromatic, 14-15, 254
Mordant, 254

Mortar and pestle, 254
Mosaic, 254
Mosaics, 191-207
    direct method, 195, 198-202
    indirect method, 195, 202-206
    suppliers, 197
    supplies, 196-97
Motif, 7, 254 (see Design)
Multiple color printing, 69-73

N

Nichrome wire, 170, 254
Nonobjective design, 10, 12, 254

O

Open design, 254
Organic, 8-9, 254
Organic material, 254
Overcast stitch, 49
Overhand knot, 88-89